Top 25 locator map

◄

TwinPack
Andalucía

DES HANNIGAN

Des Hannigan is a travel writer
and photographer who has
written numerous travel books,
including guides to Ireland,
England, Spain, Greece,
Northern Europe and North
Pakistan, many of them for
the AA.

If you have any comments
or suggestions for this guide
you can contact the editor at
Twinpacks@theAA.com

AA Publishing
Find out more about AA Publishing
and the wide range of travel publications
and services the AA provides by visiting
our website at *www.theAA.com/travel*

Contents

About this book

KEY TO SYMBOLS

✚ Grid reference to the Top 25 locator map

✉ Address

☎ Telephone number

🕐 Opening times

🍴 Restaurant or café on premises or nearby

Ⓜ Nearest underground (tube) station

🚉 Nearest railway station

🚌 Nearest bus route

⛴ Nearest riverboat or ferry stop

♿ Facilities for visitors with disabilities

✋ Admission charge

↔ Other nearby places of interest

❓ Tours, lectures or special events

▶ Indicates the page where you will find a fuller description

ℹ Tourist information

TwinPack Andalucía is divided into six sections to cover the six most important aspects of your visit to the region. It includes:

- The author's view of Andalucía and its people
- Suggested walks and drives
- The Top 25 Sights to visit
- The best of the rest – aspects of Andalucía that make it special
- Detailed listings of restaurants, hotels, shops and nightlife
- Practical information

In addition, easy-to-read side panels provide fascinating extra facts and snippets, highlights of places to visit and invaluable practical advice.

CROSS-REFERENCES
To help you make the most of your visit, cross-references, indicated by ▶, show you where to find additional information about a place or subject.

MAPS
The fold-out map in the wallet at the back of the book is a large-scale map of Andalucía.
The Top 25 locator maps found on the inside front cover and inside back cover of the book itself are for quick reference. They show the Top 25 Sights, described on pages 24–48, which are clearly plotted by number (**1** – **25**, not page number) in alphabetical order.

PRICES
Where appropriate, an indication of the cost of an attraction is given by ✋ Expensive, Moderate or Inexpensive. An indication of the cost of a restaurant is given by € signs: €€€ denotes higher prices, €€ denotes average prices, while € denotes lower prices.

ANDALUCÍA
life

A Personal View

HERITAGE IN PROGRESS
Andalucía has all the faults and foibles of any modern region. At times there is a heavy price to be paid, environmentally and aesthetically, for expansion and mass tourism. Improved communications mean that new roads slice across the landscape. Air quality in the traffic-logged streets of Granada and Seville can be very poor during the hottest months. Perhaps the best hope for this once bitterly poor region is that its astonishing beauty will survive the negative aspects of modern development as more and more people come to appreciate its heritage and landscapes.

Andalucía is the reality that matches the dream. It is a land moulded by numerous influences, from those of prehistory to classical Rome, from medieval Arabia to 20th-century civil war. Of these, the Moorish influence has been the most enduring and seductive.

The Moors conquered this southern area of Spain, which extends from the pounding surf of the Atlantic to the green rolling hills of Jerez eastward to the mountains of the Sierra Nevada, in a couple of centuries. They left their mark in a series of monuments and buildings – from Granada's Alhambra to Córdoba's Mezquita – that are wonders of the Islamic world and are intriguing reminders of a time when the world's great religions collided in southern Spain. Andalucían cities are among Spain's most vibrant and exciting, with Seville and Córdoba leading the nation in flamenco and tapas. Cadiz in the southwest corner has an air of faded glamour, while Jerez is famous for sherry, horses and an eagerly awaited annual motorcycle race.

The landscapes of Andalucía are astonishingly varied. Beneath intensely blue skies lie vast fields of golden barley and yellow sunflowers, rolling hills of red and saffron-coloured earth studded with olive trees, dramatic desert 'badlands', the green foothills of the snow-capped Sierra Nevada and the rugged cliffs of countless lesser mountain ranges. Scattered across this vivid fabric lie the great cities, dramatic 'white towns' and clifftop villages that make Andalucía so alluring.

The distant mountains of the Sierra de Cazorla

There is always an alternative here. You can enjoy the crowded high life of the Costa del Sol, find glamour and excitement in Seville and Granada, or experience the flavour of North Africa in

One of a series of secluded coves around the town of Nerja

ROADS
Andalucía's main roads were improved greatly during the late 20th century. Today you can travel quickly and comfortably on dual carriageways between most main centres. Many rural roads have been improved, although you need to be prepared for a sudden deterioration in road surfaces, especially in mountain areas.

Almería province. You can stop the world in the shade of a village plaza, become immersed in the colourful festivals of remote villages, wander through cool labyrinths of Moorish streets or stumble across little-known baroque churches and elegant Renaissance buildings in sleepy provincial towns. And you can always find solitude among the distant mountains of the Sierra Cazorla, in the green foothills of Las Alpujarras, or along the lonelier stretches of the Atlantic coast.

Andalucía can be all things to all people, provided this intriguing and evocative land is explored with an open mind and with Andalucían enthusiasm. Sunseeker, sightseer, foodie: whatever you love, Andalucía will get your heart racing. It's a thrillingly varied, beautiful region of Spain, drenched in sunlight for most of the year. Yes, parts of it have become stale with resort developments for tourists, but that's all the more reason to explore the enthralling interior where you'll receive a warm welcome from everyone, and perhaps a chilled glass of *fino* if the time is right.

Visitors admire the Muslim palace of the Alhambra in Granada

7

Andalucía in Figures

GEOGRAPHY
- Most southerly of Spain's 17 political regions or *Comunidades Autónomas* (Autonomous Communities).
- Eastern half of coastline borders the Mediterranean; western half borders the Atlantic.
- Area: 87,300sq km.
- Length of coastline: 800km.
- About one third over 600m high. Highest point: Mulhacén (3,482m), in the Sierra Nevada.
- Population: 7 million.

CLIMATE
- Typical Mediterranean climate: hot, dry summers and mild, wet winters. Atlantic coast subject to the fierce wind known as the *Levante*, and to a hot dry wind called the *Sirocco* that blows from Africa.
- Average annual temperature: 17°C; spring: 20°C; summer: 25°C; autumn: 18°C; winter: 13°C.
- Average annual rainfall: 500mm.
- Average hours sunshine each day: 9.

AGRICULTURE
- Annual production of olives: 2 million tonnes; grain: 4 million tonnes; grapes: 6.5 million tonnes.
- Other products: oranges, lemons, bananas, melons, sugar cane, tomatoes, cucumbers, peppers, potatoes, cotton, tobacco, herbs, spices and flowers.
- *Plasticultura*, the intensive production of fruit and vegetables in huge plastic greenhouses, occupies large areas of the coastal plains east and west of Almería.
- Local specialities: cured ham (Sierra Morena and Las Alpujarras); horse-breeding (Jerez de la Frontera area); breeding of fighting bulls (hill country bordering Guadalquivir river valley).

INDUSTRY
- Mainly light industry, principally located along Guadalquivir Valley.
- Concentration of engineering, food-processing and textile-production at Seville.
- Tourism is a major contributor to the economy.

People of Andalucía

Artists

Two of Spain's most famous painters, Diego Velázquez (1599–1660) and Bartolomé Esteban Murillo (1617–82) were born in Seville. Pablo Ruiz Picasso (1881–1973), one of the world's greatest artists, was born in Málaga. Picasso left Andalucía in his early teens to study in Barcelona and then in Madrid. He later moved to Paris. In Málaga, you can visit the Casa Natal Picasso, the birthplace of the artist, and the fine new Picasso Museum (➤ 40).

Musicians

Spain's most significant modern composer, Manuel de Falla (1876–1946) was born in Cádiz and lies buried in the city's cathedral crypt. Spanish folk music played a great part in de Falla's work. His most famous compositions are *Nights in the Garden of Spain* and the ballet *El Sombrero de Tres Picos (The Three-Cornered Hat)*. Unhappy with Francoism, de Falla left Spain to live in Argentina, where he died. The great Spanish guitarist, Andrés Segovia (1893–1987) was born in Linares, in Jaén province. He was made Marquis of Salobreña by royal decree in 1981 and died in Madrid.

Writers

The most famous and most tragic of Andalucía's writers was the poet and playwright Federico García Lorca (1898–1936). Lorca epitomised the passionate, intense, yet life-affirming spirit of Moorish Andalucía. He was born near Granada and his work resonated with the life of rural Spain and with Gypsy culture. Of his best works, the most noted are the plays *Blood Wedding* and *The House of Bernarda Alba*, and the book of poems *Death of a Bullfighter*. Lorca was murdered by Francoite sympathisers. His body has never been found. One of Andalucía's leading poets was Juan Ramón Jiménez (1881–1958), who was born in Moguer. His most famous work is *Platero and I*, a lyrical evocation of Moguer that he dedicated to his donkey, Platero.

NORTHERN ROMANTICS

Andalucía has attracted romantics to its 'exotic' shore since 1809, when the English poet Lord Byron visited and praised the Andalucían women. Other distinguished visitors included Washington Irving, who wrote *Tales of the Alhambra*, Hans Christian Andersen, Richard Ford, Benjamin Disraeli, George Borrow and Theophile Gautier. Modern enthusiasts included Ernest Hemingway and Gerald Brenan; the latter lived in Las Alpujarras, at Yegen (➤ 28), during the 1920s and 1930s, and wrote *South from Granada*.

The Picasso Museum in Málaga, where the artist was born

A Chronology

25,000BC	Cave paintings at Nerja and La Pileta indicate work of Late Palaeolithic hunter-gatherers.
4000–1500BC	Neolithic settlement of Southern Spain from North Africa followed by Bronze Age introduction of metal-working.
700–500BC	Colonisation by Phoenicians, then by Greeks and finally by Carthaginians.
210–151BC	Roman colonisation of Spain. Foundation of Córdoba as centre of Roman administration.
AD409	Spain is invaded by Vandals. At this time, Southern Spain may have become known to North African Muslims as 'Vandalusia'.
711BC	Muslim forces capture Gibraltar and soon dominate 'al-Andalus'.
784	Work begins on mosque at Córdoba.
1031	Al-Andalus fragments into separate kingdoms.
1086	The Almoravids, a powerful Islamic sect, take control of al-Andalus.
1146	Almohads, independent Muslims with roots in Berber society, come to dominate al-Andalus.
1163	Seville becomes the capital of al-Andalus. Building begins on the Giralda tower in 1184.
1236	The Christian King Fernando III captures Córdoba from the Moors.
1237	Granada becomes the centre of a shrinking Moorish Andalucía. The building of the Alhambra begins.
1248	Fernando III captures Seville from the Moors.
1469–1489	The marriage of Fernando (Ferdinand) of Aragón and Isabel (Isabella) of Castile. Fernando and Isabel capture Málaga, Baeza and Almería.

1492	Unification of Spain completed.
1568–70	*Moriscos* (Moors who had 'converted' to Christianity) rebel against Christian rule. Las Alpujarras becomes a Morisco area of refuge.
1609–11	Last remaining *Moriscos* are expelled from Spain.
1704	British capture Gibraltar.
1834	Andalucía is divided into eight provinces.
1924–1931	King Alfonso XIII forced to share rule of Spain with dictator Miguel Primo de Rivera. Alfonso XIII goes into exile. Second Republic proclaimed.
1936–9	Civil War between incumbent Republicans and Nationalist rebels ends in victory for Nationalist forces under General Franciso Franco. Franco's long dictatorship begins.
1968	Border with Gibraltar is closed by Spain.
1975	Death of Franco. Juan Carlos I, the grandson of Alfonso XIII, becomes king.
1982	The Sevillian politician Felipe González becomes Prime Minister of Spain at head of first Socialist government since the Civil War. Andalucía becomes an Autonomous Community with its own Parliament in Seville and administered by a regional government: the Junta de Andalucía.
1985	Reopening of border between Spain and Gibraltar.
1992	World Exhibition (EXPO) held in Seville.
2003	The Museu Picasso opens in the artist's birthplace, Málaga.
2007	The first stage of Málaga airport's major expansion plan is completed, as the second stage (another terminal and runway) gets underway.

Best of Andalucía

If you only have a short time to visit Andalucía, and are looking for the best way to experience the essence of the region, here are some suggestions for activities and places that shouldn't be missed.

- Visit the world-famous attractions, in spite of the crowds: Seville's cathedral and Giralda (➤ 51), Granada's Alhambra (➤ 27), Córdoba's Mezquita (➤ 38), make sure you take in the Alcazabas of Almería (➤ 25) and Málaga (➤ 26), as well.
- Check to see whether there is a local festival in the area you are visiting. If there is, make sure you attend. Be ready to party.
- Always take time to relax at a café table while watching the world go by.
- Visit the *pueblos blancos*, the 'white towns' and hilltop villages of Málaga and Cádiz province, such as Zahara de la Sierra (➤ 48), Grazalema (➤ 53), Arcos de la Frontera (➤ 52) and Vejer de la Frontera (➤ 53).
- Go for a long walk in Las Alpujarras (➤ 28), the Sierra de Grazalema, the Sierra Morena or the Sierra de Cazorla (➤ 20–21).
- See some flamenco at a classical performance venue, at a festival, or at a *Peñas Flamencas*, a flamenco club. Ask at local tourist offices for details.
- Eat Andalucían. Try gazpacho, a delicious cold soup that comes in several forms, but always based on cucumber and tomatoes with olive oil and wine vinegar. Eat fish anywhere, but especially in Cádiz. Above all, indulge yourself in *jamón serrano* or *pata negra*, the delicious cured ham of the Sierras; and sip *fino*, the driest and finest of sherries, as you go.
- Try to visit at least two or three of the following: Jerez de la Frontera (➤ 36), Priego de Córdoba (➤ 43), Baeza (➤ 29), Úbeda (➤ 47).
- Browse in village shops that are off the tourist trail. You will find some fascinating items that do not carry 'souvenir' prices.

Palm trees line the promenade in the town of Nerja

ANDALUCÍA
how to organise your time

A Walk Along the Guadalquivir

INFORMATION

Distance 2km
Time 1 hour 30 minutes
Start/end point Follow
  instructions for the Sierras
  drive (➤ 18) to turning at
  junction signed Coto Rios;
  keep right here, signed
  Parador de Turismo. There's
  a café and seating at the
  base of the hill. At next
  junction keep left, signed
  Vadillo Castril. Soon, at a
  wide area, reach a junction
  with a road bending sharply
  right. Keep ahead for about
  100m to a parking space
  on the right, just before a
  small house
Lunch Parador de Cazorla
  (€€€)
  ✉ Sierea de Cazorla s/n
  ☎ 953 72 70 75

A short walk through dramatic mountain scenery alongside the infant Río Guadalquivir.

From the parking space, walk downhill to reach a bridge over the Río Guadalquivir. Don't cross the bridge, but turn left along a rocky path.

The Guadalquivir was first named Betis by the Romans, then Guad al Quivir (The 'Great River'), by the Moors. It rises in the heart of the Sierra de Cazorla and flows through Andalucía for 657km to the sea at Sanlúcar de Barrameda (➤ 73).

Follow the rocky path as it rises along the side of the river valley. Descend steeply and go down winding steps to reach a weir. Go down steps to the base of a waterfall that drops from the weir.

The valley widens here and is flanked on either side by great cliffs. Brightly coloured dragonflies and damselflies flit across the river pools.

Continue along the path beneath overhanging cliffs. There are shaded seats alongside the path.

Swifts dip and weave through the sky from their nests in the looming rocks above. Keep an eye open for mountain goats, which often graze at these lower levels.

Soon the path leads above a deep wooded valley and reaches a superb viewpoint just beyond an old wellhead and water pipe. Continue along a track through trees and keep left on the main track. At the next junction go right to reach a road and large parking area beside a notice board. Turn left and go downhill for a short distance to the parking space.

The Sierra de Cazorla, beautiful hiking country

The Barrio Santa Cruz, Seville

This is a basic tour of the Barrio's old Jewish quarter; you can divert at will down numerous alleyways on the way.

From Plaza Virgen de los Reyes walk up Calle Mateos Gago and at the junction go right down Mesón del Moro. At the junction with Ximenez de Encisco go left, then right down Cruces to a small square.

At the centre of the square are three slightly incongruous columns, the most conspicuous survivors of Roman Seville.

Leave the square by its left-hand corner and go down Mariscal into Plaza de Refinadores. (You can divert into the Jardines de Murillo here.) Go right, across the back of the Plaza, then down Mezquita into Plaza de Santa Cruz.

Just off Plaza de Santa Cruz is Calle Santa Teresa. The Museo de Murillo at No 8 traces the life of painter Bartolomé Esteban Murillo (1617–82), who lived there.

Leave Plaza de Santa Cruz by its left–hand corner and enter Plaza Alfaro. Go right along Lope de Rueda, then right to reach Reinosa. Go left, then left again at Jamerdana to Plaza de los Venerables.

There are guided tours (daily 10–2, 4–8) of the Hospicio de los Venerables Sacerdotes, which has a marvellous patio and superb paintings.

Leave the Plaza along Gloria lane to reach the Plaza Doña Elvira. Leave by the Vida and go into Judería. Turn right, then go through vaulted archways to Patio de Banderas. Cross the square and go under the archway to Plaza del Triunfo and the cathedral.

INFORMATION

Distance 1.5km
Time About 3 hours, with visits to museums
Start/end point Plaza Virgen de los Reyes
🟦 B2
Lunch Hosteria de Laurel (€€)
✉ Plaza de los Venerables
☎ 954 22 02 95

Exploring the Barrio Santa Cruz, Seville

A Walk Through Old Cádiz

A walk through the narrow streets of the old town, visiting museums and one of Cádiz's most remarkable churches on the way.

INFORMATION

Distance 2.5km
Time About 3 hours, with visits to museums and churches
Start/end point Plaza San Juan de Dios
➕ A3
Lunch El Machleño (€–€€)
✉ Plaza de Mina

From the far corner of the Plaza San Juan de Dios, to the right of the Town Hall, go along Calle Pelota and into Plaza de la Catedral. Leave by the far right-hand corner of the Plaza and go along Compaña to the busy Plaza de la Flores. Leave the Plaza to the left of the post office building to reach the market square, La Libertad.

Plaza de la Flores is surrounded by fine buildings overlooking a flower market. The food market in La Libertad is in full swing in the mornings.

Leave the market square along Hospital de Mujeres. Turn right along Sagasta and continue to Sta Ines. Go left here and pass the Museo Iconográfico e Histórico to reach the Oratorio de San Felipe Neri. From the church, go down San José, crossing junctions with Benjumeda and Cervantes, then left through Junquería into Plaza de San Antonio.

A myriad of narrow cobbled streets make up the old town of Cádiz

This vast square edged with seats is a pleasant place to relax in the sunshine.

Leave the Plaza on the same side as you entered, but go down Ancha, then go left along San José to Plaza de Mina and the Museo de Cádiz (► 39). Take Tinte, to the right of the museum, to Plaza de San Francisco. From the square's opposite corner follow San Francisco through Plaza de San Augustín and on down Calle Nueva to Plaza San Juan de Dios.

A Drive Through Las Alpujarras

Challenging roads, the Sierra Nevada's prettiest villages and Spain's highest mountain – this drive has something for driver and passengers alike.

Take exit 164 off the Motril-Granada motorway (A44), signed La Alpujarra. Follow the road uphill until you are higher than the wind turbines on the hillsides. Lanjarón is the first town. Go through the town and at the first roundabout take the right exit for Orgiva to continue on the A348. Go straight over the next roundabout as you leave Lanjaron. Continue on the A348 towards Orgiva. Before you enter the town, turn left after the petrol station onto the A4132 to Trevélez.

Continue to Pampaneira, ignoring all turn-offs. The landscape gets greener and more wooded up here. Before you reach Pampaneira you'll cross the Río Poqueira gorge. Pass through Pampaneira and take the next left signposted for Bubión.

Whitewashed Bubión, overlooking the gorge, is one of the most popular Alpujarran villages. Beyond the next village, Campileira, the road peters out at the foot of Mulhacén, Spain's highest mountain at 3,479m.

Return downhill to the junction with the A4132 through several mountain towns, following signs to Trevélez and Ugijar. You're now entering the high Sierra Nevada and Mulhacén's snow-streaked peak will fill your windscreen.

At Trevélez, the highest village in Spain, stay on the A4132 – the road veers right. At the top, follow the road to the left for Juviles, which becomes the A4130. At Juviles, bear right and head downhill to the foot of the hill. Turn right, signposted Orgiva. At the next junction, turn right again for Orgiva, rejoining the A348, which offers stunning views of Las Alpujarras.

The next village is Cadiar; keep left to stay on the A348 to Orgiva. At Orgiva, stay left, following signs for Lanjarón. At Lanjarón, turn left for the A44 Granada-Motil highway.

INFORMATION

Distance approx 100km
Time 4 hours (not including stops)
Start/end point exit 164 off Granada-Motril road (A44)
🚪 C3
Lunch La Artesa, Bubión (➤ 64)

17

A Drive Through the Sierras

This is quite a long drive with a great deal to see. An overnight stop at somewhere like Segura de la Sierra is worthwhile.

INFORMATION

Distance 214km
Time 8 hours
Start end/point Úbeda
🔁 D2
Lunch Café de la Corredera (€€)
✉ Plaza de la Corredera 18, Cazorla
☎ 953 72 01 02

From Úbeda, go east along the N322, signed Valencia, Albacete. After 2km, bear right, signed Cazorla. Watch carefully for a Halt sign and at a roundabout, take the exit signed A315, Cazorla.

The road winds pleasantly towards distant mountains through low hills covered with olive trees. Fields of wheat and barley shine like gold in early summer.

At the main square of Cazorla (► 53), go round the roundabout and take the higher road marked 'Sierra' on its surface and signed for Parque Natural. Pass La Iruela village, where a ruined castle stands on a rock pinnacle. At Burenchal take the right fork, signed Parque Natural. Follow the winding A319 through magnificent scenery. After 15km, go left at a junction signed Coto Ríos.

The old Moorish castle, La Yerda, dominates Cazorla from on high

The road follows the Guadalquivir valley through beautiful wooded mountains, passes the visitors' centre at Torre del Vinagre, then runs alongside the Tranco reservoir.

Two-thirds of the way along the reservoir, cross a dam and keep right at the junction. After 9km, at a junction below the hilltop village of Hornos, go left, signed Cortijos Nuevos. Go through Cortijos and at the roundabout take the second right, signed La Puerta de Segura. Continue on the A317 and follow signs for La Puerta de Segura and Albacete. Drive carefully through Puerta de Segura, then follow signs for Puente de Genave and Úbeda. Join the N322 and return to Úbeda.

Exploring the Pine Mountains

A short drive from Ronda through the spectacular mountain roads of the Parque Natural Sierra de Grazalema.

Leave Ronda, from the north, following signs to Seville and the A374. Stay on the A374 as it drops into the valley, rises again and passes through a gorge. Take the road through the Sierras, the A372, left from the A374 – and stay on the A372 to Grazalema.

The road winds down towards the village, past overhanging roadside crags where you may see rock climbers inching their way up the faces.

Continue through Grazalema and in a few kilometres turn off right at a junction (signed Zahara de la Sierra).

This spectacular mountain road through the Sierra Margarita climbs to the Puerta de Palomas Pass, at 1357m. The mountains are covered in a mix of *pinsapo* pine, a rare species found only in the Grazalema area, cork oak and holm oak. You may see an eagle drifting over the high ground.

Once over the pass, the road follows a series of spectacular hairpin bends that demand concentration. At Zahara de la Sierra (▶ 48), drive as far as the central square, go round its central point, then bear right and follow narrow streets downhill through the one-way system. At the base of Zahara turn left, signposted A339 for Ronda. Continue down to the Arroyomolinos recreation and then follow the road right, along the edge of the reservoir for Ronda. (Left takes you to Seville and Jerez.) At the junction with the A376, turn right and return to Ronda.

INFORMATION

Distance 85km
Time 6 hours, with stops
Start/end point Ronda
✚ B3
Lunch Los Naranjos (€–€€)
✉ c/San Juan 15, Zahara de la Sierra
☎ 956 12 33 14

The village of Grazalema cuts a swathe through the mountains

19

Finding Peace & Quiet

Andalucía is such a large and varied region that opportunities for escaping the crowds are plentiful. Although the best places to find peace and quiet are in the hills and mountains of the interior, there are also large areas of undeveloped coastline to the east and west of the Costa del Sol.

COASTAL NATURE PARKS AND RESERVES

The coastal section of the distinctive Parque Natural de Cabo de Gata-Nijar is centred on the cape that makes up the eastern arm of Almería Bay. The waters off Cape Cabo de Gata have recently seen the reintroduction of the endangered Mediterranean monk seal. Las Salinas, the area of salt pans just south of the village of Cabo de Gata, is noted for its thousands of migratory birds in spring and autumn. Parque Nacional Coto de Doñana lies on the Atlantic seaboard to the west of Cádiz, and comprises the vast area of dunes and marshland of the delta of the River Guadalquivir. The Parque is one of Europe's largest and most important wetland areas, with over 250 bird species recorded.

INLAND NATURE PARKS AND RESERVES

Parque Natural Sierra Maria is a large area of rugged limestone mountains near Vélez Blanco (► 53) in Almería province, with a rich cover of aleppo pines, larch and Scots pines. It harbours rare plants, eagles and butterflies, and offers

TURISNAT
The park services in the Parque Natural de Cazorla, Segura y Las Villas operate a range of activities, including 4x4 tours of the park and wildlife watching.
✉ TurisNat Paseo del Cristo 17, Cazorla ☎ 953 72 13 51, www.turisnat.org

The clear waters of Cabo de Gata attract snorkellers and divers

Popular with walkers, El Torcal is one of Andalucía's most spectacular natural parks

excellent walking opportunities. Desierto de las Tabernas is famous for its use in the Clint Eastwood 'Spaghetti Western' films. The wider area is a semi-arid region of sculpted hills and gulches lying to the north of Almería. It has some unique plants and animals, and surprising oases of palm trees. It can be mercilessly hot.

Cork trees rise from the sun-bleached grass of a plantation in the Spanish countryside

The scenically spectacular Parque Natural Sierra de Grazalema is an area of mountains and wooded lesser hills surrounding the villages of Grazalema (➤ 53) and Zahara de la Sierra (➤ 48). One of the last refuges of the Spanish pine, the *pinsapo*, it is a superb walking and rock-climbing area, and is reputed to have the highest annual rainfall in Spain, so there's a possibility of cooling off.

Located inland from Tarifa, the Parque Natural de los Alcornocales harbours one of the world's largest areas of cork oak forest. There is a chance of spotting golden eagles, vultures, roe deer and red deer.

The Parque Natural Sierra Nevada, a huge area of high land southeast of Granada, contains the highest mountains in Andalucía, with Mulhacén its highest peak. The southern foothills of the area, Las Alpujarras (➤ 28), offer delightful walking opportunities through wooded valleys and terraces. The higher slopes are more rugged and dramatic.

The Parque Natural Sierras de Cazorla, Segura y Las Villas is a marvellous area of mountains and forests, within which the River

The unique wetlands of the Coto Donaña National Park

Guadalquivir has its modest source. Located in the northeast of Jaén province, this is the largest area of protected wilderness in Andalucía, with a great sense of remoteness off the beaten track. Griffon vultures, golden eagles, red deer and Spanish ibex are only a few of the more dramatic creatures to be seen here.

What's On

JANUARY	6 Jan: *Cabalgata de los Reyes Magos*, Málaga. Epiphany parade.
FEBRUARY	Pre-Lenten, week-long *Carnaval* in many Andalucían towns and cities: mid-month.
MARCH	*Semana Santa*, Holy Week. Follows Palm Sunday and is one of the most passionate celebrations in the world. Most colourful and dramatic in Seville.
APRIL	Month of the most exuberant *ferias*, that of Seville being considered the best and biggest in Spain. Held one or two weeks after Easter, but always in April. Vejer de la Frontera holds an Easter Sunday *feria*, with bull-running through the streets.
MAY	First week: Horse Fair, Jerez de la Frontera. *Fiesta de las Patios*. Córdoba's fabulous private patios are open to the public in early May. *Romería del Rocío*. Whitsun. Vast numbers congregate at the village of El Rocío, Huelva, to celebrate *La Blanca Paloma*, the 'White Dove', the Virgen del Rocío. *Corpus Christi*. Thursday after Trinity Sunday. Festivals and bullfights; Seville, Granada, Zahara de la Sierra and at smaller towns and villages.
JUNE	Second week: *Feria de San Barnabé*. Marbella. 13–14 Jun: *San Antonio Fiesta*. Trevélez, Las Alpujarras. Mock battles between Moors and Christians.
JULY	*La Virgen del Carmen*. Fuengirola, Estepona, Marbella Nerja and Torremolinos. Celebrates the patron saint of fishermen.
AUGUST	5 Aug: *Mulhacén Romería*, Trevélez. Midnight procession to Sierra Nevada's highest peak. 13–21 Aug: *Feria de Málaga*. Very lively fiesta. Mid-Aug: horse-racing; Sanlúcar de Barrameda. Races along the sandy beaches. Third weekend: *Fiesta de San Mames*, Aroche. Friendly village fiesta.
SEPTEMBER	7 Sep: *Romería del Cristo de la Yedra*, Baeza. Street processions and entertainment. First two weeks: *Pedro Romero Fiestas*, Ronda. Celebration of famous bullfighter.
OCTOBER	15–23 Oct: *Feria de San Lucas*, Jaén. The city's main festival. 6–12 Oct: *Feria del Rosario*, Fuengirola. Horse riding and flamenco.
DECEMBER	28 Dec: *Fiesta de los Verdiales*. Lively, theatrical and musical event in villages to the north of Málaga.

ANDALUCÍA's
top 25 sights

The sights are shown on the maps on the inside front cover and inside back cover, numbered **1**–**25** alphabetically

The Albaicín, Granada

*A water fountain in Plaza
Nueva (above)*

*Houses of the Albaicín
(below)*

**An intruiging maze of narrow, cobbled
lanes, the Albaicín is Granada's old
Moorish neighbourhood and many
original Moorish buildings remain.**

Granada's antidote to its modern city streets is
the engaging Albaicín, the old Moorish quarter
that occupies the northern side of the valley of
the Río Darro and the hill of Sacromonte, the
city's much vaunted Gitano, or Gypsy quarter.

The Albaicín is best reached from Plaza
Nueva by following the Carrera del Darro, past
the Baños Árabes and the Museo Arqueológico
(► 54) and on beyond the attractive terrace of
Paseo de los Tristes, where there are numerous
cafés in the shade of the Alhambra Hill. You can
plunge into the heart of the Albaicín by going
along the Carrera del Darro and its continuation
of Paseo del Padre Manjón, and then by turning
left up Cuesta del Chapiz. Part of the way up,

the Camino del Sacromonte
leads off right into the Gypsy
quarter and the notorious
'flamenco caves', where you risk
off-loading large sums of money
to watch insistent but not
entirely authentic flamenco
shows.

The real pleasures of the
Albaicín lie in the maze of streets
and marvellous local plazas with
their bars and restaurants. Find
your way to the famous Mirador
de San Nicolás for a world-
famous sunset view of the
Alhambra; but hang on to your
bag, very tightly – the local
thieves are absolute masters at
spiriting   away   anything
moveable the minute it is
put down.

La Alcazaba de Almería

Step back into the Moorish conquest of Andalucía with a trip to the Alcazaba, an impressive Moorish fort above Almería.

INFORMATION

🔋 D3
✉ Almanzor s/n
☎ 950 17 55 00
🕐 Nov–Apr daily 9–6.30;
　 Apr–Nov daily 9–8.30
🍴 Bar/café (€€)
♿ Few
💶 Inexpensive; free with
　 EU passport

La Alcazaba dominates Almería, although the modern town seems oddly detached from it. The happily scruffy Barrio de Chanca, a district of brightly painted, flat-roofed houses, surges up to its walls. An entrance ramp winds steeply up to Puerta de las Justicia (the Justice Gate), unmistakeably Moorish in style. Beyond is the First Precinct, cleverly renovated and reflecting, in its gardens and water channels, what the original must have been like. The views over the city are superb.

A gentle climb past flowering shrubs and tinkling water leads to a beautiful oasis of trees hard against the walls of the Second Precinct. Here marble slabs, inscribed with verses by García Lorca and Fernando Villalon, rest against the wall. Inside the Second Precinct are the foundations of Moorish bathhouses. The Third Precinct encloses the triangular fortress, originally Moorish but greatly strengthened by the Christians. The views are breathtaking.

Across the broad valley of San Cristóbal to the west is the Mirador de San Cristóbal, linked to the Alcazaba by the Muralla de San Cristóbal, a distinctive fortified wall.

Stepped, cremellated walls of the Alcazaba (above)

A patchwork of fields sits below the walls of the Alcazaba fortress (left)

25

3

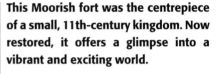

La Alcazaba de Málaga

INFORMATION

➕ C3

✉ Calle Alcazabilla s/n

☎ 952 12 88 30

🎦 Museo de la Alcazaba
Tue–Sun 9.30–8

🍴 El Jardin, Calle Canon
(€–€€)

🚌 35

♿ None

♿ Inexpensive; free Sun
after 2pm

*Sunset glows on the
ancient stone walls of
the Gibralfaro (above)*

*Alcazaba is shadowed by
the Castillo de Gibralfaro
(below)*

This Moorish fort was the centrepiece of a small, 11th-century kingdom. Now restored, it offers a glimpse into a vibrant and exciting world.

Málaga's Alcazaba has a wonderful sense of antiquity in its rough walls and in the maze of terraces, gardens, patios and cobbled ramps that lead ever upwards through impressive archways into the sunlight. The lower part of the Alcazaba dates from the 8th century, but the main palace is 11th-century.

Málaga's long history is reflected in the partly excavated Roman theatre, below the entrance to the Alcazaba, and in the various marble classical columns embedded within the dark brickwork of the fortress. The upper palace contains the small Museo de la Alcazaba, which displays Moorish artefacts recovered from the site and vicinity, amid decorative patios and rooms. Views of Málaga from the ramparts of the Alcazaba are magnificent.

Adjoining the Alcazaba and connected by the long, honey-coloured city walls, the Gibralfaro castle is accessed via tropical gardens to the right of the Alcazaba. The castle was constructed in the 14th century but was still being used during the Spanish Civil War of the 1930s. There are great views of the Alcazaba from the castle's battlements.

La Alhambra

La Alhambra is the greatest surviving expression of Moorish culture in Spain, and is one of the world's most spectacular heritage sites.

The Alhambra stands on top of Granada's Sabika Hill, against the background of the Sierra Nevada. The walled complex is nearly 700m long and 200m wide. Its name is a corruption of the Arabic *Al Qal'a al-Hamrá*, the red castle, a reference to the ruby-red sandstone walls of the Alcazaba, the original fortress built on Sabika by the 11th-century Emirs of Córdoba. The Alhambra's other Islamic buildings were established during the 13th and 14th centuries by the Nasrites.

There are four distinct groups of buildings within the Alhambra: the Alcazaba; the Casa Real, the 14th-century Royal Palace of the Sultans; the Palace of Carlos V, a late 15th-century Renaissance addition; and the Palacio del Generalife, the gardens and summer palace of the Sultans.

Viewing the Alhambra may take a day and there are usually crowds. The heart of the Alhambra is the Casa Real, which reflects the ingenious manipulation of space and light and of cool water that was the special gift of Moorish architecture. The walls and roofs of its salons display exquisite stucco work, tiling and decorations that will take your breath away.

Adjoining the Casa Real is the unfinished Palacio de Carlos V, an impressive example of High Renaissance architecture. To the west of here is the fortified Alcazaba, an older, more rugged monument than the domestic buildings of the Casa Real. From the Alcazaba's Vela tower there is a spectacular view of Granada. At the eastern end of the Alhambra complex, on *Cerro del Sol*, the Hill of the Sun, lies the luxurious Generalife, a captivating world of tinkling fountains and mirrored pools.

INFORMATION

- C3
- Calle Real s/n
- 902 44 12 21; www.alhambra-patronato.es
- Mar–Oct daily 8.30–8; floodlit visits Tue–Sun 10pm–11.30pm. Nov–Feb 8.30–6; floodlit visits Fri, Sat 8pm–9.30pm
- Drinks and snack kiosk
- Alhambrabus every 10 minutes: Plaza Isabel la Católica–Plaza Nueva
- Few
- Expensive (free to visitors with disabilities and senior citizens); free Sun after 3pm
- Even out of season, it is recommended to book your Alhambra entry, as numbers are restricted. Tickets can be reserved up to one year ahead by phoning 902 22 44 60 (in Spain) or 0034 915 37 91 78 (from abroad). You can also book via any branch of Spain's BBBV bank. The main ticket gives free-ranging access to Alcazaba, Generalife and Carlos V Palace; it is marked with a half-hour time slot permitting entry to the Casa Real. The International Festival of Music and Dance takes place at various venues throughout the Alhambra from the end of June to early July

Las Alpujarras

INFORMATION

➕ C3
✉ Southern Sierra Nevada,
  Granada province
🍴 Bars and restaurants in
  most villages (€–€€)
🚌 Granada–Alpujarras
  ☎ 958 18 54 80
❓ Fiesta de San Antonio,
  Trevélez, 13–14 Jun.
  Pilgrimage to the peak of
  Mulhacén from Trevélez,
  5 Aug

The southern foothills of the Sierra Nevada, known as Las Alpujarras, were the last stronghold of Moorish influence in medieval Spain.

The hills of Las Alpujarras descend in green waves to the arid river valleys of the Río Guadalfeo in the west and the Río Andarax in the east. On the south side of these valleys lie the Sierra de Contraviesa and the Sierra de Gádor, mountain barriers that shut out the populous and developed Almerían coast. A more ancient people than the Moors first carved out cultivation terraces and irrigation channels on the hillsides, but the region's history as the final enclave of the *Moriscos*, nominally Christianised Moors, has given Las Alpujarras much of its romantic appeal.

This is complex and enchanting countryside, which offers superb walking. Driving in Las Alpujarras can also be a pleasure, provided you accept that it may take you all day to drive 50km along the great shelf of hills. Narrow, serpentine roads bend to the terraced slopes and sink discreetly into the valleys. Ancient villages and hamlets such as Bayárcal, Yegen and Bérchules invite relaxing halts. The flat-roofed, North African-style houses of the villages are painted white now, but originally the bare stone walls merged with the landscape.

At the heads of the deepest western valleys in the 'High Alpujarras' lie popular villages

Trees rise before the Berber-style village of Bubión (top) in the valley of Las Alpujarras (above)

such as Trevélez, 'capital' of *jamón serrano*, the famous cured ham of the mountains. Further west is the Poqueira Gorge, a deep valley striking into the heart of the Sierra Nevada. Clinging to its slopes are the charming villages of Pampaneira, Bubión and Capileira, from where the wild country of the Sierra is easily reached on foot.

Baeza

Baeza is one of several towns in the Andalucían heartland where evidence of Roman, Moorish and Christian settlements has been preserved.

Renaissance elegance and style is the hallmark of Baeza's old quarter, where remnants of long years of Moorish influence have been replaced with 16th-century classical buildings of the highest order. The busy central Plaza de España extends into the tree-lined Paseo de la Constitución, with its lively pavement bars and cafés.

The town's Renaissance treasures lie on the higher ground, east of here. At the southern end of the Paseo de la Constitución is the handsome Plaza de los Leones, also known as Plaza del Pópulo, with its central fountain and double-arched gateway, the Puerta de Jaén.

Steps (Escalerillas de la Audienca) lead from the tourist office, then left to Plaza Santa Cruz, where you will find the Palace of Jabalquinto, with its superbly ornamented Gothic façade. The Renaissance courtyard and glorious baroque staircase are currently in poor condition, but are being refurbished. Opposite the palace is the delightful little Romanesque church of Santa Cruz, with traces of the earlier mosque that it supplanted.

The Cuesta de San Felipe leads uphill from Plaza Santa Cruz to Plaza de Santa María, the magnificent heart of Renaissance Baeza. The plaza is dominated by Baeza's massive 13th-century cathedral, which has an exhilarating 16th-century nave. At the centre of the square is a fountain in the form of a rustic triumphal arch, behind which stands the 16th-century seminary of San Felipe Neri, its walls bearing elegant graffiti.

INFORMATION

🔲 D2
✉ 48km northeast of Jaén
🍴 Numerous restaurants and bars (€–€€€)
🚌 Daily, Jaén–Baeza, Granada–Baeza, Úbeda–Baeza
🚆 Railway station at Linares–Baeza, 14km from Baeza; connecting buses
🏛 Plaza del Pópulo s/n
☎ 953 74 04 44
♿ Few
🎉 Semana Santa, Mar/Apr. Romería del Cristo de la Yedra, 7 Sep

Decorative arches enclose a pretty corner of Baeza (above). People gather outside the 16th-century cathedral (below)

Barrio Santa Cruz, Seville

INFORMATION

➕ B2

✉ East of cathedral

🍴 Great mix of bars, cafés
and restaurants (€–€€€)

♿ Few

Packed with funky bars and restaurants, Seville's Santa Cruz quarter has beautiful squares, narrow streets and superb spots for people-watching.

A first experience of the tightly-knit alleyways of the Barrio Santa Cruz can seem claustrophobic. Tall buildings shut out the sun; their stonework is dark and gloomy; the mood seems more northern European than Andalucían. But the Barrio eventually captivates.

Santa Cruz was the *aljama*, or Jewish quarter, of the medieval city and was greatly changed after the Jewish community was expelled in 1492. The area was much restored and refurbished in the first years of the 20th century, and its narrow, muffled streets are a wonderful antidote to the raging traffic of Seville's busy main thoroughfares. Whether you wander at will or follow a plan, soon you will discover flower-filled corners such as Plaza Santa Cruz, the Jardines de Murillo on the Barrio's eastern boundary, and the Plaza Doña Elvira. There are numerous bars and cafés in which to take a break along the way.

It's a delight to stroll the tight network of alleyways known as Barrio Santa Cruz (top and above)

Many of the streets and squares, which were restored in the 1920s, have a story attached to them. For example, Plaza Alfaro inspired the balcony scene in Rossini's *Barber of Seville* opera. Next to Plaza Alfaro is one of the prettiest squares in the neighbourhood, Plaza Santa Cruz – the church of Santa Cruz stood in this square before it was demolished in 1810 by the French. The church is now on Calle Mateos Gago, close to the new Arab hammam on Calle Aire. Note that the whole of Barrio Santa Cruz can become congested in the summer peak season with sightseers; spring and autumn are more comfortable times to visit and you'll be able to find a table outside too.

Carmona

Delightful Carmona stands majestically on a high escarpment overlooking the fertile valleys of the Río Corbones and the Río Guadalquivir.

Over 4km of ancient walls enclose old Carmona, and the main entrances to the town are through magnificent Roman gateways, the Puerta de Sevilla and the Puerta de Córdoba. The lively and sun-drenched Plaza de San Fernando, circular and fringed by trees, has some eye-catching buildings, and near by is the spacious market, a big patio enclosed by arcades.

Follow the narrow Calle Martín López de Córdoba out of Plaza de San Fernando to reach the church of Santa María la Mayor. The church is entered through the delightful Patio de los Naranjos, the entrance patio of the mosque that originally stood here, still with its orange trees and horseshoe arches. The church has a soaring Gothic nave and powerful *retablo*. Uphill, Calle G Freire leads to Carmona's superbly located Alcazar del Rey de Pedro, now an exclusive *parador* (state-run hotel).

The Seville Gate incorporates the Moorish Alcazar de Abajo, where Carmona's helpful tourism office is located. Beyond the gate, across the busy Plaza Blas Infante, is modern Carmona, dominated by the handsome church of San Pedro, whose great tower replicates the style of Seville's Giralda and which has a wonderful baroque sacristy. A wide and busy promenade leads to Carmona's Roman Necropolis, a beautifully preserved series of dramatic burial chambers and one of the most remarkable archaeological sites in Andalucía.

INFORMATION

- ➕ B2
- ✉ 30km west of Aracena; 38km east of Seville
- 🚩 Arco de la Puerta de Sevilla ☎ 954 19 09 55; www.turismo.carmona.org
- 🍴 Several bars, cafés and restaurants (€–€€)
- 🚌 Daily, Seville–Carmona
- ♿ Few
- ❓ Carnival, Feb. Holy Week

Roman Necropolis

- ✉ Avda de Jorge Bonsor 9
- ☎ 954 14 08 11
- 🕐 Mid-Jun to mid-Sep Tue–Sat 9–2, Sun 10–2; mid-Sep to mid-Jun Tue–Fri 9–5, Sat–Sun 10–2
- 💵 Free with EU passport

The bell tower of Santa María (top). Whitewashed walls line the streets of Carmona (above)

La Casa de Pilatos, Seville

INFORMATION

- B2
- Plaza Pilatos 1
- 954 22 52 98
- Daily 9–7 (winter until 6)
- Bodega Extraména, Calle San Esteban (€€)
- C1, C2, C3, C4 (for Plaza San Agustin)
- Small ferry boats from nearby resorts
- Few
- Expensive

Fountains and azulejos *decorate a shady patio (above and below)*

The Casa de Pilatos is an enthralling illustration of how Seville's wealthiest residents lived, packed with art from the owners' travels. But it is the building that is the real star.

The Casa de Pilatos (Pilatos House) is one of Seville's finest treasures. Built in 1519, the house was said to be a copy of Pontius Pilate's house in Jerusalem, but there is no real evidence confirming this. The entire building is a glorious celebration of the Mudéjar style mixed with the most elegant of Italianate features. To have such sustained Mudéjar design in one building is a delight. The *azulejos* tiling is outstanding; the patios, arcades, stairways and richly furnished salons are all superb. As an experience, this is the best place to truly get a feel for the subtle complexities of this unique architecture. There is hardly a finer self-contained complex of late medieval style and design in all of Andalucía.

Commissioned by the Ribera family after a journey to Jerusalem, the Casa de Pilatos contains an assortment of artworks and treasures from around the world. There are paintings by the Spanish artists Goya and Valdés, a superb fresco, the *Apotheosis of Hercules*, by Francisco Pacheco (in a room of its own on the upper floor), and sculptures and busts from Greece and Italy. The gardens and patios, too, suffused with the scent of orange trees and decorated with statues, pools and little enclaves, are similarly stunning and probably represent the best in Seville.

Écija

The town of Écija, dating from Roman times, is a real hotspot – the plains around it swelter in summer. Visit in spring or autumn to best appreciate its elaborate towers and churches.

This Ciudad de las Torres (City of Towers) is all dramatic skyline. Eleven magnificent church towers, steepled, domed and exquisitely decorated with colourful tiles, punctuate the sky, each with its resident storks.

The town is much more than its towers. There are 18th-century façades, so fluid in their forms that they hint at the work of Barcelona's Antoní Gaudí. The Palacio de Peñaflor in Calle Castellar is a fine building, painted and sinuous and with a flamboyant baroque portal, lacking only a wider street to set if off. The Palacio de Benameji in Calle Cánovas del Castillo, home to the tourist office, is another delight. The splendid central square, the Plaza Mayor, or Plaza de España has been walled off for the construction of an underground car park, which has robbed the encircling arcades and pleasant cafés of light and air; all the more reason to admire the glorious church towers.

INFORMATION

🔲 B2
✉ 80km east of Seville
🍴 Several bars, cafés and restaurants (€–€€)
🔲 Daily, Seville–Écija
🛈 Plaza de España 1
☎ 955 90 29 33;
www.turismoecija.com
♿ Few
❓ Holy Week. Feria de Primavera (Spring Fair), 8 May

The Iglesia de Santiago in Écija (below)

Gibraltar

INFORMATION

➕ B3

✉ 120km southwest of Málaga

🍽 Several bars, cafés and restaurants (€€–€€€)

🚌 Daily, Cádiz–La Linea, Málaga–La Linea; regular buses La Linea–Gibraltar

♿ Good

The minuscule colony of Gibraltar, in a corner of Andalucía, is forever British. The monkeys, and the Rock which they patrol, are the chief attraction.

The wide open spaces of the airport approach to Gibraltar emphasise just how spectacular the famous 'Rock' is. This is the genuine point of contention between Spain and Britain, steeped in nautical history. Gibraltar has been a British colony since 1704 and, although its populace has evolved into an engaging mix of British-Mediterranean character, the buildings, culture, style and especially the commerce are emphatically British.

Gibraltar is a curiosity: it's a place where British expats can shop in familiar High Street shops for specifically British products and then return to their holiday homes on the Costa del Sol. However, holidaymakers will be more interested in the Rock of Gibraltar, a wave-shaped cliff at the gateway to the Mediterranean. Here, watch out for the bold and bad-tempered Barbary apes (technically they're monkeys), which pester visitors for food.

There is enough in Gibraltar to make a visit enjoyable, apart from just the fascination of the mighty rock: its famous apes, the cable car, St Michael's Cave and views to Africa.

Gibraltar has long been prized for its strategic position at the mouth of the Mediterranean, with Phoenicians, Moors and the British maintaining it as an outpost. For many years Spain has desired the return of Gibraltar to Spanish hands and there are regular campaigns for it to rejoin Spain, although these are resisted by Gibraltar's inhabitants. But for now, you will still have to show your passport at the police and customs post when you enter.

St Michael's Cave (top)

Barbary apes have made the rock their home (above)

Gruta de las Maravillas, Aracena

The spectacular limestone formations of Aracena's underground cave system, the Gruta de las Maravillas, are the finest in Andalucía.

Aracena's limestone caves, the Gruta de las Maravillas (Grotto of Marvels, or Cavern of the Wonders) comprise nearly 1.2km of illuminated galleries and tunnels that are open to the public. These galleries link 12 spectacular caverns, where limestone deposits have formed stalactites and stalagmites and densely layered flows of calcium carbonate known as tufa. There are six small lakes within the system and the whole is linked by walkways, ramps and steps. Carefully arranged lighting adds to the effect and piped music, specially written for the site, murmurs in the background. (Note the caves can be quite chilly.)

Guided tours of the caves are accompanied by commentary in Spanish, but non-Spanish speakers will still enjoy a visually stunning experience. Stay near the back of the crowd and you will have time to admire the fantastic natural architecture that often seems to mirror, with grotesque exaggeration, the intricate decoration of baroque altars and Mudéjar façades of Andalucían churches. The caverns all have special names, and the guide points out lifelike figures and faces on the convoluted walls and roofs. The final cavern, known famously as the *Sala de los Culos*, the 'Room of the Backsides', is exactly that: a hilarious extravaganza of comic rude bits, of huge limestone phalluses and entire tapestries of pink tufa buttocks. You will hear groups of elderly Spanish ladies at the head of the throng shriek with laughter as they reach this part of the tour.

INFORMATION

- A1
- Pozo de la Nieve s/n
- 959 12 82 06
- Daily 10.30–1.30, 3–6; Mon–Fri tours every hour. Sat–Sun tours every half-hour
- Restaurante Casas (€€)
- Daily Huelva–Aracena, daily Seville–Aracena
- None
- Moderate
- Tickets booked at the tourist centre opposite caves' entrance. At busy times your entry time may be an hour or two ahead

Aracena's underground cave system (above and below)

13

Jerez de la Frontera

➕ A2

✉ 35km northeast of Cádiz, 83km south of Seville

🍴 Numerous restaurants and bars (€–€€€))

🚉 Estación de Ferrocarril Plaza de la Estacion s/n

🚌 Estación de Autobuses, Plaza de la Estación
   ☎ 956 34 52 07

♿ Few

ℹ Calle Larga
   ☎ 956 32 47 47;
   www.turismojerez.com

❓ Semana Santa (Holy Week). Horse Fair, early May, Vendemia, wine festival, early Sep

Jerez de la Frontera has given its name to sherry, one of the most popular drinks in the world. It is also a centre of equestrianism and flamenco.

The rich chalky soil of the Jerez area supported vine-growing from the earliest times. Today, the coastal region that lies south of a line between Jerez and Sanlúcar de Barrameda (► 73) is the official sherry-producing area, the Marco de Jerez. The famous sherry-producing bodegas of Jerez are where fermented wine, produced mainly from white Palomino grapes, is stored and transformed into sherry, and where brandy is also produced. Tours of bodegas end with a pleasant tasting session, confirming the precise distinctions between dry *Fino* and the darker and sweeter *Oloroso* and *Amontillado*.

Jerez's other famous institution is the Real Escuela Andaluza del Arte Ecuestre (Royal Andalucían School of Equestrian Art) at Avenida Duque de Abrantes: the horse-riding displays should not be missed. Jerez has excellent cafés, restaurants and shopping, especially in its pedestrianised main street Calle Larga. Rewarding visits can be made to the restored 11th-century Alcázar and Arab Baths, the delightful Plaza de la Asunción and the Barrio Santiago, Jerez's old Gypsy or *gitano* quarter, with its narrow lanes and old churches. In the Barrio you can visit the Museo Arqueológico (Archaeological Museum) in Plaza del Mercado and see archive material and audio-visual presentations about flamenco, at the Centro Andaluz de Flamenco in the Plaza de San Juan.

Horsemen enter the cobbled yard at the School of Equestrian Art (top). Jerez's 11th-century Alcázar (above)

Judería, Córdoba

Córdoba's medieval Jewish quarter, the Judería, surrounds the Mezquita and is a wonderful place to explore on foot, with plenty of bars and cafés.

The engaging maze of narrow alleys that lies between the Plaza Tendillas and the Mezquita is the Judería, Córdoba's old Jewish quarter. The area of the Judería close to the Mezquita is given over to souvenir shops, but there is still much charm in popular venues such as the flower-decked Callejón de las Flores, a narrow cul-de-sac whose walls neatly frame the Mezquita's old minaret tower. At CalleMaimónides 18, near the Museum of Bullfighting, there is a 14th-century synagogue, the only one in Andalucía and a good example of Mudéjar architecture. Near the synagogue is the Puerta de Almodóvar, a 14th-century city gate flanked by a statue of the Roman scholar Seneca, who was born in here.

The Judería is a good starting point for any tour of central Córdoba, with several large car parks on the far side of the main roads ringing this part of the old town. The neighbourhood, which is accessed by several gateways *(puertas)*, is bordered on one side by a river which is now dry for most of the year, although the Romans bridged it with a now-restored series of arches.

INFORMATION

➕ C1

🍴 Numerous bars, cafés and restaurants (€€–€€€)

ℹ️ Calle Torrijos 10
    ☎ 957 47 12 35

Clay pots filled with flowering geraniums adorn the whitewashed walls of the Judería (above and below)

15

La Mezquita, Córdoba

INFORMATION

🔲 C1
✉ Calle de Torrijos 10
☎ 957 47 12 35
🕐 Apr–Sep Mon–Sat 10–7,
  Sun 2–7; Oct–Mar
  Mon–Sat 10–5, Sun 2–7
🍴 Restaurante Bandolero
  Calle de Torrijos 6 (€€)
🚉 Estación de Ferrocarril,
  Avenida de América
♿ Few
🎫 Moderate

*Inside the Mezquita
(above). Your carriage
awaits outside the
Mezquita (below)*

**Of all the wonderful Moorish build-
ings to survive in Andalucía, the Great
Mosque of Córdoba is the most haunting, as well as the most Islamic in
its forms.**

The Mezquita (Mosque) of Córdoba was begun
in 785 and expanded and embellished during
the following two centuries. You enter the
complex by the Patio de los Naranjos, the
Courtyard of the Orange Trees, where numerous fountains once sparkled in the dappled
shade and where Moslem worshippers carried
out ritual ablutions.

The mosque itself is then entered through
the modest Puerta de Las Palmas. Immediately,
you are amid the thickets of columns and arches
that are the enduring symbol of the Mezquita.
Smooth pillars of marble, jasper and onyx,
plundered from the building's Roman and
Visigothic predecessors, supplement the total of
over 1,200 columns supporting the
horseshoe arches of red brick and white
stone. At the far end of the vast interior
you will find the *mirhab*, the prayer niche
of the mosque, a breathtaking expression
of Islamic art.

At the very centre of the Mezquita
stands the 1523 Renaissance cathedral of
Carlos V, an intrusion that reflected
Christian pride rather than piety. Carlos
later admitted that the addition of the
cathedral had 'destroyed something
that was unique in the world'.
The cathedral's presence is cloaked by the
surrounding pillars of the mosque and made
somehow less obvious, although it is the focus
of worship today. Its carved mahogany choir
stalls are outstanding, but it is the Islamic
Mezquita, with its forest of columns and
swirling arches, that is most compelling.

Museo de Cádiz

Cádiz's fascinating seafaring history is explored in the city's museum, one of the most interesting in Andalucía. Phoenicans, Romans and Moors all left their mark on Cádiz.

Cádiz is one of the great historic ports of the Mediterranean, with a claim to being the oldest of European cities, and a distinctive peninsular site lending it immense character. The city wa founded as *Gaadir* by the mineral-seeking Phoenicians, who exploited the tin and copper of the Sierra Morena. Under later Moorish control, the city declined, and even today that distinctive Andalucían Moorishness seems absent from Cádiz. During the 18th century, the decline of Seville as a river port benefited Cádiz and the city became rich on the Spanish-American gold and silver trade.

The Museo de Cádiz (Cádiz Museum) is the pride of Cádiz and one of the best museums in Andalucía. It is distributed around a central patio, and the museum's three sections explore Phoenician and Roman culture to Spanish painting from the 16th century. The ground-floor collection is outstanding, especially the Roman displays where a wreck of a Roman boat is used to illustrate all the commodities shipped out of Cádiz during that era. Also on the ground floor, look out for a pair of Phoenician marble sarcophagi, produced during the 5th century BC and the only examples found in the western Mediterranean.

On the first floor are paintings by Roger van der Weyden, Murillo, Rubens and Zurbarán – there are 21 works by Zurbarán, including a collection of saints he painted while travelling around the Carthusian monasteries of Spain, such as La Cartuja in Jerez de la Frontera (► 36). The top floor has displays of craftwork and a collection of traditional marionettes.

INFORMATION

➕ A3
✉ Plaza de Mina 5
☎ 956 20 33 68
🕐 Tue 2.30–8, Wed–Sat 9–8, Sun 9.30–2.30
🍴 Cervecería Gaditana, Calle Zorilla (€€)
🚌 2
♿ Few
🎟 Inexpensive; free with EU passport

Exhibits from the Phoenician collection (above)

Museo Picasso, Málaga

INFORMATION

✚ C3

✉ Palacio de Buenavista,
Calle San Agustin 8

☎ 902 44 33 77; www.
museopicassomalaga.org

🕐 Tue–Thu 10–8, Fri–Sat
10–9

💶 Moderate

Andalucía's most famous artist was born in Málaga, but it wasn't until 2003 that Picasso was celebrated with his own purpose-built museum in the city.

The long-awaited Picasso Museum eventually opened its doors in October 2003, and this innovative, informative venue was certainly worth the wait. Housed in the handsome 16th-century Palacio de Buenavista, the splendid museum contains a collection of more than 200 Picasso works, including paintings, drawings, sculptures, engravings and some fine ceramics. Some archaeological remains can be viewed in the basement.

The core, permanent collection was donated by Picasso's daughter-in-law and grandson, Christine and Bernard Ruiz-Picasso, while works loaned from other major museums contribute to the temporary exhibitions. While you won't find many of Picasso's most famous works, the museum provides an insight into the private life and background of one of the world's most famous artists. The Projection Room on the ground floor sheds light on his production processes. There is also an auditorium and reading room on the ground floor, for a more detailed study of the man and his work.

This beautiful palace plays host to the Picasso Museum (top). Enter through the huge stone entrance and discover the world of Picasso (right)

Parque Natural el Torcal

El Torcal with its spectacular rock formations is 13km south of the town of Antequera and is one of the most remarkable of Andalucía's Natural Parks.

The limestone pinnacles and cliffs of the Sierra del Torcal cover an area of 1,171ha. The name *Torcal* derives from the word for 'twist' and aptly sums up the maze of narrow vegetation-filled gullies and ravines among the towering reefs and pillars of rock. From the visitors' car park there are several waymarked circular walking routes through the labyrinth. The shortest route tends to be crowded, but there are longer circular routes, and well-worn paths into the labyrinth can be followed, and then retraced. An early morning or late afternoon visit is recommended.

The dense undergrowth is formed from holm oak, hawthorn, maple and elder; ivy clings to the rock faces. Flowering plants include saxifrage, peony, rock buttercup, rock rose and numerous species of orchid. El Torcal's general isolation supports a rich bird life that includes the great grey shrike, vultures and eagles, as well as many small perching birds. There is a good chance of spotting the fierce-looking ocellated lizard, the largest lizard in Europe.

A reception centre at the entrance to El Torcal has an exhibition and audio-visual display with excellent information about the geology and wildlife of the area. Exhibits are labelled in Spanish only. A short path leads from near the reception centre to the Mirador de las Ventanillas, a spectacular viewpoint.

INFORMATION

- ✚ B3
- ✉ Centro de Recepcion, Parque Natural el Torcal, Antequera
- ☎ 95 20 313 89
- 🕐 Reception Centre, daily 10–5
- 🍴 Café (€€)
- ♿ Few

Bizarre limestone rock formations created by the ravages of wind and rain (above and below)

Plaza de España, Seville

INFORMATION

➕ B2
✉ Avenida de Isabel la
Católica
🍴 La Raza, Isabel la Católica
2 (€–€€)
🚌 C1, C2, C3, C4
♿ Good
ℹ Paseo de las Delicias 9
☎ 954 23 44 65

Catch your breath in the tranquil surroundings of the María Luisa Park and the grand Plaza de España, lying east of the city, on the Guadalquivir river.

Seville's remarkable Plaza de España and the María Luisa Park were the crowning glories of the city's ill–fated 1929 Ibero-American Exhibition, a grandiose event that failed to measure up to expectations. The Plaza and park are, however, great legacies. The Plaza is a huge semicircular complex of buildings lined with colourful motifs in *azulejos* tiling and fronted by a short length of canal, spanned by ornamental bridges. The María Luisa Park is a glorious stretch of wooded gardens, drenched in flowering plants. Beyond are the Museo Arqueológico (Archaeological Museum) and the Museo de Costumbres Populares (Popular Arts Museum), both fascinating.

A horse-drawn carriage in the dappled shade of the Parque de María Luisa (top)

An arched bridge spans the canal, with Plaza de España in the background (above)

The Museo Arqueológico occupies the plaza's most impressive buildings. It has 27 rooms dedicated to Andalucían history, from Palaeolithic periods up to and including the Moorish conquests. It's the sort of museum that prompts more questions than it answers, with a mysterious collection of 6th-century gold treasure (the Carambolo Treasures) that may point the way to the long-lost land of Tartessus. In the Roman galleries there are several rooms filled with artefacts recovered from digs across Andalucía. Make time to see at least the exterior of the Museo de Costumbres Populares; while the collections inside are rather incoherent, the building itself, a Mudéjar pavilion with beautiful tilework, is spectacular.

Priego de Córdoba

The charming Córdoban town of Priego de Córdoba is rich in baroque architecture and offers a rare insight into provincial Andalucía.

From Priego's central square, the handsome Plaza de la Constitución, the broad Calle del Río leads southeast past the churches of Our Lady of Anguish and Our Lady of Carmen to a peaceful square containing two splendid fountains. These are the 16th-century Fuente del Rey, with its handsome sculpture of Neptune and Amphitrite, and the more restrained Renaissance fountain, the Fuente de la Virgen de la Salud.

From busy Plaza Andalucía, adjoining the Plaza de la Constitución, walk northeast down Solana and through the Plaza San Pedro to a junction with Calle Doctor Pedrajas. To the left is a 16th-century slaughterhouse, the Carnicerías Reales, beautifully preserved with an arcaded patio, from where a superb stone staircase descends to a basement. Turning right along Calle Doctor Pedrajas brings you to the Plaza Abad Palomina and the privately owned Moorish Castillo. Priego's greatest baroque monument, the Iglesia de la Asunción (Church of the Ascencion), is at the far corner of the square. Its plain, whitewashed exterior gives no indication of the treasures inside, a beautifully carved *retablo* (altarpiece) and a spectacular *sagrario* (sacristy), an extravaganza of white stucco, frothing with emblems and statues beneath a cupola pierced by windows.

From delightful little Plaza de Santa Anna, alongside the church, head into the Barrio de la Villa down Calle Real, and wander through the maze of this old Moorish quarter, bedecked with flowers. Stroll along Calle Jazmines to find the Paseo de Adarve, an airy Moorish promenade with superb views to the surrounding hills, an elegant final flourish to Priego's charms.

INFORMATION

- C2
- 65km southeast of Córdoba, 60km northwest of Granada
- Numerous restaurants and bars (€–€€€)
- Granada–Priego, Córdoba–Priego, Estación de Autobuses, Calle San Marcos
- Carrera de las Monjas 1 Mon–Sat 10–2, 4–7, Sun 10–2 957 70 06 25; www.turismodepriego.com
- Few

Looking down on the Fuente del Ray fountain, a feature of the town (above)

Reales Alcázares, Seville

INFORMATION

🔷 B2

✉️ Patio de Banderas

☎️ 954 50 23 23; www.
patronato-alcazarsevilla.es

🕐 Apr–Oct Tue–Sat 9.30–7,
Sun 9.30–5; Oct–Mar
Tue–Sat 9.30–5, Sun
9.30–1.30

🍴 Numerous cafés and
restaurants in
surrounding streets
(€–€€€)

🚌 C1, C2, C3, C4

ℹ️ Avenida de la
Constitución 21B ☎️ 954
11 14 04/954 21 81 57

♿ Few

💰 Moderate; children under
12 and senior citizens free

❓ A visit early or late in the
day may win you some
added space. At busier
times, numbers are
regulated and you may
have to wait your turn

The Royal Palaces of Seville are a superb example of Mudéjar-style building, displaying Moorish-influenced post-Conquest architecture.

After Seville fell to Christian forces in 1248, the Spanish king Pedro the Cruel reshaped and rebuilt much of the city's original Alcázar in Mudéjar style. It is this version that survives at the heart of the present complex, in spite of many restorations and in spite of the often clumsy additions made by later monarchs.

Highlights of the Alcázar include the Chapel of the Navigators, where Isabella of Castile masterminded the conquest of the Spanish Americas. The room's coffered wooden ceiling is studded with golden stars. Inside the palace is the Patio of the Maidens, with fine stucco work and *azulejos* tiling. Beyond lies the Salón de Carlos V, with superb *artesonado* ceiling and then the Alcázar's finest room, the Salon of the Ambassadors, crowned by a glorious dome of wood in green, red and gold and with a Moorish arcade.

Adjoining the main palace are the dull and cavernous chambers of the Palacio de Carlos V, added by that insatiable intruder upon fine buildings, the Habsburg king. These lead to the serene gardens of the Alcázar, where an arc of water from a high faucet crashes spectacularly into a pool in which a bronze statue of Mercury stands in front of a rusticated façade: the Gallery of the Grotesque. The rest of the gardens are a pleasant conclusion before you emerge into the Patio de las Banderas, with Seville's cathedral beckoning ahead.

Iglesia de Santa Maria, on Plaza de Vazquez de Molina (above). Inside the Reales Alcázares (left)

Ronda

Surrounded by mountains and with a spectacular gorge, Ronda is one of the prettiest of Andalucía's whitewashed villages – and the most visited.

The dominant feature of picturesque Ronda is the deep gorge (El Tajo) of the Río Guadalevín. Between its towering walls, a handsome 18th-century bridge, the Puente Nuevo, hangs like a wedge, groaning beneath the massed weight of visitors. On the south side of the bridge is the charming old Moorish town. Its focus is the Plaza Duqueza de Parcent, where the fine Iglesia de Santa María Mayor stands on the site of an original mosque. The church has strong Gothic and baroque features, but numerous Moorish elements survive to add an exotic flair. Other places to visit south of the gorge include the Palacio de Mondragón in Calle Manuel Montero, the Minaret de San Sebastian in Calle Armiñan, the Iglesia del Espíritu Santo close to the Puente Nuevo and the well-preserved Arab Baths near the Puente Viejo, or Old Bridge, to the east.

INFORMATION

- B3
- ✉ 118km northwest of Málaga
- 🍴 Numerous bars, cafés and restaurants (€–€€€)
- 🚆 Daily, Málaga–Ronda
- 🚌 Daily, Málaga–Ronda. Seville–Ronda
- ℹ Plaza España 1 ☎ 952 87 12 72
- ♿ Few
- ⁈ Holy Week, Feria y Fiestas de Pedro Romero, 31 Aug–10 Sep (traditional bullfighting)

Ronda's centrepiece spans the El Tajo gorge (above). Inside the bullring (below)

Sierras de Cazorla, Segura y Las Villas

INFORMATION

- D2
- 90km northeast of Jaén
- Bars, cafés and restaurants (€–€€)
- Twice daily, Cazorla–Torre del Vinagre–Cotos Rios
- Paseo del Santo Cristo 17 ☎ 953 71 01 02; Parque Natural Information Centre, Calle Martinez Falero 11, Cazorla ☎ 953 71 15 34
- Few

Centro de Interpretación Torre del Vingre

- Torre del Vinagre
- ☎ 953 71 30 17
- Summer daily 10–2, 5–8.30; spring and autumn daily 11–2, 4–7; winter Tue–Sun 11–2, 4–6

This sprawling natural park has a wealth of wildlife and rugged scenery, making it the best wilderness area in Andalucía.

The Sierras of Cazorla, Segura and Las Villas make up the largest of Andalucía's Parque Naturales (Natural Parks), at an impressive 214,000ha. The mighty Río Guadalquivir has its modest source here, amid spectacular rocky mountains that support great swathes of oak and pine woods. The Sierras are a complex of deep valleys and high ridges, with the mountain of Las Empanadas being the highest point at 2,107m. This is a winter landscape of snow and ice, but in late spring, summer and autumn the Sierras are delightful, often hot and sunny, yet verdant, with higher than average rainfall for such terrain. There are good opportunities for short or long walks, and you can also book trips in off-road Land Rovers.

There is a wealth of wildlife in these mountains. Over 1,000 plant species include the Cazorla violet, unique to the area. Trees include the black pine, Aleppo pine and evergreen oaks, and there is a multitude of animals large and small, including fox, wild cat, polecat, otter, deer, mountain goat and wild boar. Birds include griffon vulture, booted and golden eagles, peregrine falcon and kite. At Torre del Vinagre (▶ 18), 34km northeast of Cazorla, there is an interpretation centre. Adjoining the centre is a rather morgue-like Museo de Caza, a hunting museum, and nearby is a botanical garden. Land Rover trips and mountain bike or horse rides can be booked at the visitor centre.

Sierra de Segura (above). Isolated buildings dwarfed by the vast mountain slopes (left)

Úbeda

Although famous for its Moorish architecture, Andalucía also boasts some of Spain's finest Renaissance buildings. Úbeda has some of the best.

Renaissance Úbeda survives triumphantly within its more modern and often featureless surroundings. To reach the crowning glory of the Plaza de Vázquez de Molina, you need to navigate the urban maze from the town's modern centre at the busy Plaza de Andalucía. From here the narrow Calle Real runs gently downhill to the Plaza del Ayuntamiento, where a short street leads to the glorious enclave of Plaza de Vázquez de Molina. Just before entering the Plaza, you will find, on the right, Úbeda's remarkable Museo de Alfarería (Pottery Museum), which is well worth a visit.

On the right as you enter Plaza de Vázquez de Molina is the Palacio de las Cadenas, the work of the great classical architect Andrés Vandelvira. Directly opposite is the handsome Church of Santa María de los Reales Alcázares, enclosing a lovely Gothic cloister on the site of an original Moorish building. East of here lie other fine buildings, culminating in a 16th-century palace, now Úbeda's luxurious Parador hotel (▶ 70).

At the east end of the Plaza is the Sacra Capilla del Salvador. This private burial chapel dates from the mid-16th century and was completed by Vandelvira to an earlier design. The grand exterior apart, inside you will find a carefully restored *retablo* (altarpiece) of breathtaking splendor, beneath a soaring cupola. Other fine buildings and churches are found in Plaza San Pedro, reached from halfway down Calle Real, and in Plaza del Primero de Mayo, just north of Plaza de Vázquez de Molina.

INFORMATION

* D2
* 45km northeast of Jaén
* Numerous restaurants and bars (€–€€€)
* Daily, Jaén–Úbeda, Granada–Úbeda, Baeza–Úbeda
* Palacio del Marqués del Contadero, Calle sp Majo Marqués 4
* ☎ 953 75 08 98; www.andalucia.org
* Few
* Fiesta de San Miquel, 4 Oct

Renaissance façades fringing the Plaza de Vázquez (above)

Palacio de las Cadenas (below)

Zahara de la Sierra

- ✚ B2
- ✉ 22km northwest of Ronda
- 🍽 Restaurants and bars (€–€€)
- 🚌 Daily, Ronda–Zahara de la Sierra
- ℹ Plaza de la Rey 3
  ☎ 956 12 31 14
- ♿ Few
- ❓ Corpus Christi, end May–early Jun

Hailed as one of the finest of the *pueblos blancos* ('white towns') of Ronda, Zahara de la Sierra occupies a spectacular hilltop position.

The red-roofed, white-walled houses of the lovely village of Zahara cluster beneath a dramatic hilltop castle at the heart of the Sierra Margarita in the Parque Natural Sierra de Grazalema. Below, to the northeast, is a large reservoir, the Embalse de Zahara, formed by damming the Río Guadalete. Zahara's castle has Roman origins, but was rebuilt by the Moors during the 12th century. It was later occupied by Christians, and its reckless retaking by the forces of Granada's Nasrid rulers in 1481 prompted Ferdinand and Isabella to launch the final conquest of Moorish Granada and its province.

If you visit Zahara by car, it is best to find a roadside parking space near the top of the steep approach road before entering the centre of the village. Zahara is a delightful hilltop enclave, its Moorish character intact. The castle has been recently renovated and is reached from the village square by following a winding pathway uphill past a charming cave fountain. The views from the castle and its tower are spectacular, but take care on the steep, unlit steps. The tiny village square stands in front of the baroque church of Santa María de la Mesa, and there is an airy *mirador*, viewing balcony, overlooking the reservoir. At the other end of the main street, at the entrance to the village, is the little church of San Juan, which harbours some vivid statues. At night, Zahara's castle is floodlit and its centre and side streets take on a charming intimacy.

The delightful 'white town' clustered beneath a Moorish castle (top and above)

ANDALUCÍA's
best

Churches

In the Top 25
🔟 LA MEZQUITA, CÓRDOBA (➤ 38)

CATEDRAL NUEVA

The massive Catedral Nueva (New Cathedral) in Cádiz is still under restoration, but open to the public; check opening times before visiting. The building dates from the prosperous 18th century, and replaced the 'old' cathedral of Santa Cruz. The neoclassical main façade on Plaza de la Catedral is magnificent. It is crowned by a baroque dome, famously 'gilded' yet, in reality, faced with glazed yellow tiles. The interior of the cathedral is a gaunt, stone cavern, classically perfect; below lies the claustrophobic crypt, which contains the grave of the musician Manuel de Falla.

➕ A3 ✉ Plaza de Mina 5, Cádiz ☎ 956 28 61 54 🕐 Tue –Fri 10–1.30, 4.30–6.30, Sat 10–1 🍽 Café bar La Marina, Plaza de Las Flores (€€) 🚌 4 ♿ Few 🎟 Inexpensive; free with EU passport

Granada's 16th-century cathedral

CAPILLA REAL

The Capilla Real (Royal Chapel) was built between 1506 and 1521 as a sepulchre for Los Reyes Católicos, Fernando and Isabel, one of the most terrifying double acts in history. The Gothic Royal Chapel is an odd mixture of the flamboyant and the constrained. It is impressive, yet lacks entirely the subtle elegance of Moorish buildings. The most striking feature of the chapel is the altar's superb *retablo* (alterpiece), a gilded extravaganza. In the sacristy are displayed, among royal heirlooms, Isabel's splendid collection of paintings by Flemish masters and others.

➕ C3 ✉ Oficios 3, Granada ☎ 958 22 92 39 🕐 Apr–Oct Mon–Sat 10.30–1, 4–7, Sun 11–1, 4–7; Nov–Mar Mon–Sat 10.30–1, 3.30–6.30, Sun 11–1, 3.30–6.30 🍽 Bar–Restaurante Sevilla, Calle Oficios 12 (€€) 🚌 1, 3, 4, 6, 7, 8, 9 ♿ Few 🎟 Inexpensive

CATEDRAL, ALMERÍA

Almería's cathedral seems more fortress than church. Its stark and formidable walls were built to repel the pirates and disaffected *Moriscos* (Christianised Jews) who haunted the coast in the aftermath of the Christian Reconquest. Look for the cheerful yet unexplained sun symbol on the east wall, at the entrance to the charming little Plaza Bendicho. A door in the south wall leads to a sunny little Renaissance courtyard, brimming with shrubs and flowers.

➕ D3 ✉ Plaza de la Catedral, Almería 🕐 Mon–Fri 10–5, Sat 10–1 🍽 Bodega Montenegro, Plaza Granero (€€) 🚌 Parque de Nicolás Salmerón ♿ Few 🎟 Inexpensive

CATEDRAL, GRANADA

Granada's cathedral stands near the apex of the busy junction of Gran Vía de Colón and Calle Reyes Católicos. The building dates from the 16th century and reflects all the contemporary certainties that raised it in place of a demolished mosque.

➕ C3 ✉ Gran Vía de Colón 5, Granada ☎ 958 22 29 59 🕐 Mon– Sat 10.30–1.30, 4–7, Sun and public hols 4–7 🍽 Vía Colona, Gran Vía de Colón 13 (€€) 🚌 1, 3, 4, 6, 7, 8, 9 ♿ Few 🎟 Inexpensive

CATEDRAL, MÁLAGA

Málaga's cathedral gets a bad press, due perhaps to its lack of a companion for its solitary tower. Another tower was planned originally, but was never built. The cathedral has a strong visual appeal, however, its dark, worn stonework making a pleasing contrast to the more modern buildings that crowd round it. The *coro*, or choir, is the cathedral's great glory: its fine mahogany and cedar wood stalls are embellished by carved statues of 40 saints. The adjoining church has a Renaissance high altar that will take your breath away.

➕ C3 ✉ Calle Molina Larios s/n, Málaga ☎ 952 22 84 91
🕐 Cathedral: Mon–Fri 10–6, Sat 10–5.45. Closed Sun. Iglesia del Sagrario: daily 9.30–12.30, 6–7.30 🍴 El Jardín, Calle Canon 1 (€–€€) ♿ Few 💷 Inexpensive

LA CATEDRAL Y LA GIRALDA

Seville's cathedral and its adjoining Giralda tower are among some of the most visited monuments in Europe. At busy times, the weight of people seems to diminish the grandeur of it all and, in the Giralda, especially, the climbing of the tower's 34 ramps and 17 final steps becomes something of a weary trudge. The cathedral is said to be the largest Gothic church in the world. It replaced a Muslim mosque, and was a gesture of unashamed Christian triumphalism. Outstanding works of art and religious artefacts fill the cathedral, and the alleged tomb of Christopher Columbus makes an eyecatching theatrical piece. The Giralda, the surviving 12th-century minaret of the original mosque, was heightened in 1565 by the addition of a bell tower. Views from its upper gallery are impressive.

➕ B2 ✉ Plaza Virgen de los Reyes, Seville ☎ 954 21 49 71; www.catedralsevilla.es 🕐 Mon–Sat 11–5, Sun 2.30–6 (summer 9.30–4) 🍴 Numerous bars, cafés and restaurants in Calle Mateos Gago (€–€€€) 🚌 Avenida de la Constitución ♿ Few 💷 Moderate; free Sun

MONASTERIO DE SAN JERÓNIMO

The 16th-century Convento de San Jerónimo (Convent of St Jeronimo) lies in Granada's university district. The focus of the convent is its central patio, a superb example of mixed Gothic-Renaissance features and with refreshingly peaceful cloisters, where the mellow chanting of the nuns at prayer can often be heard. The adjoining church has an inspiring interior, all painted frescoes and with a glorious four-storeyed *retablo* (altarpiece) within an octagonal apse.

➕ C3 ✉ Rector López Argueta 9, Granada ☎ 958 27 93 37
🕐 Mon–Sun 10–2.30, 4–7.30 🍴 Numerous cafés in adjoining San Juan de Dios (€) 🚌 5 ♿ Few 💷 Inexpensive

ORATORIO DE SAN FELIPE NERI

Of all Cádiz's churches, the Oratorio de San Felipe Neri is the most impressive. In March 1812, the building saw the temporary setting up of the Spanish parliament, or Cortes, that proclaimed the first Spanish Constitution – a radical document whose liberal principles were to influence European politics as a whole. Plaques on the outer wall commemorate leading Cortes deputies. Inside, two tiers of balconies above exuberant chapels complement the high altar and its Murillo painting, *The Immaculate Conception*, all beneath a sky-blue dome.

➕ A3 ✉ Calle Santa Inés 38, Cádiz ☎ 956 21 16 12 🕐 Mon–Sat 10–1.30 🍴 Freiduría Las Flores, Plaza de las Flores (€€) 🚌 2 ♿ Few 💷 Inexpensive

MONASTERIO DE LA CARTUJA

The Monasterio de la Cartuja (Monastery of the Carthusians) lies some way from Granada's city centre, but is well worth the journey. It is the most extravagant of Spain's Carthusian buildings and dates from the early 16th century. The Cartuja's monastery and church face each other across an attractive patio. The church is a lavish torrent of baroque sculpture, all swirling marble and jasper and gilded frescoes.

➕ C3 ✉ Calle Real de Cartuja ☎ 958 16 19 32 🕐 Apr–Oct Mon–Sat 10–1, 4–8; Nov–Mar daily 10–1, 3.30–6.30 🚌 8 C 💷 Inexpensive

Monasterio de la Cartuja, in Granada's Triana district

Andalucía's Best

Hilltowns & Villages

In the Top 25

🔢 **CARMONA** (➤ 31)
🔢 **RONDA** (➤ 45)

ARACENA

Aracena's most lauded attraction is the limestone cave complex, the Gruta de las Maravillas (Grotto of Marvels, ➤ 35). But Aracena and its surroundings have much to offer above ground. The town surrounds a hilltop medieval castle ruin and its adjacent church of Nuestra Señora de los Dolores; there are pleasant bars and cafés in the surrounding streets. About 20km south of Aracena, along the scenic A479, is Minas de Río Tinto and the desolate yet compelling landscape of the area's open-cast mines, where copper, silver and iron have been mined for thousands of years.

➕ A1 ✉ 89km northwest of Seville 🍴 Several (€–€€) 🚌 Daily from Seville and Huelva

ALHAMA DE GRANADA

On the lip of a rocky gorge, Alhama de Granada has a down-to-earth charm that complements its splendid old buildings. The town was a significant Moorish settlement due to its hot springs, the *al hamma*. The town's main square, the Plaza de la Constitución, is a pleasant place in which to enjoy good *tapas* at surrounding bars. Near by is the Iglesia del Carmen, a late medieval church with a lovely stone fountain outside. On the far side of the Iglesia del Carmen is a terrace overlooking the gorge of the Río Alhama.

➕ C3 ✉ 40km southwest of Granada 🍴 Café-Bar Andaluz, Plaza de la Constitución (€) 🚌 Granada–Alhama de Granada, every weekday 🛈 Calle Vendederas ☎ 958 36 06 86 ♿ Few

ARCOS DE LA FRONTERA

This is one of Andalucía's liveliest towns. It has outgrown its Moorish hilltop settlement and now spills down from the craggy heights. The older, upper part of Arcos is a maze of narrow streets that twist and turn round the two main churches of Santa María de la Asunción and San Pedro. The former dominates the central square of Plaza del Cabildo, from whose *mirador* there are stunning views of the plain below.

➕ B2 ✉ 50km northeast of Cádiz 🍴 Numerous bars, cafés and restaurants (€–€€€) 🚌 Daily, Cádiz–Arcos, Jerez de La Frontera–Arcos 🛈 Plaza del Cabildo ☎ 956 70 22 64 ♿ Few ❓ Holy Week. Easter bull-running. Feria de San Miguel, end Sep

AROCHE

This charming hilltop village lies 24km from the border with Portugal. Its Moorish castle, originally established in the 9th century, was rebuilt substantially in 1923 and now incorporates one of Andalucía's most eccentric bullrings and the village's archaeological museum. The café-bars in the main square, Plaza de España, are delightful places to while away a few hours, watching the world go by.

➕ A1 ✉ 33km west of Aracena 🍴 Bars and cafés in main square (€) 🚌 Daily, Aracena–Aroche ♿ None ❓ Holy Week. Pilgrimage of San Mamés , Whitsun. Feria de Agosto, Aug. Pilgrimage, Jun

BAÑOS DE LA ENCINA

This engaging little hilltop village rises from vast acres of olive fields. Baños has a lovely Gothic-Renaissance church in its tiny central Plaza de la Constitución, but the village is dominated by its well-preserved, 10th-century Moorish castle. The views from the top are magnificent. Resist the challenge to walk round the

A church in the hillside village of Aracena

inner, unprotected parapet if you do not have good
footwork and a head for heights.

🚻 C1 ✉ 100km east of Córdoba 🍴 Restaurante La Encina, Calle
Ambulatorio 1 (€) 🚌 Daily, Córdoba–Bailén, Úbeda–Bailén; local bus
connections between Bailén and Baños 🛈 Avenida José Luís Messías 2
☎ 953 61 32 66 ♿ Few

CAZORLA

This busy town, 'gateway' to the Parque Natural de
Cazorla, Segura y Las Villas (► 21), nestles below the
looming cliffs of the Peña de los Halcones. Plaza de la
Corredera, Cazorla's more sedate square, is surrounded
by cafés and shops. From its far right-hand corner, the
narrow Calle Nubla leads past the viewpoint of Balcón
del Pintor Zabaleta, for fine views of Cazorla's ruined
Moorish castle and Renaissance church. Plaza Santa
María below is a great place to eat and drink.

🚻 D2 ✉ 32km southeast of Úbeda 🍴 Cafés/restaurants (€–€€)
🚌 Daily from Granada, Jaén and Úbeda 🛈 Paseo del Santo Cristo 17
☎ 953 71 01 02 ♿ Few ❓ Pilgrimage to La Virgen de la Cabeza,
last Sun/Mon in Apr

GRAZALEMA

Mountains define Grazalema. They loom like clouds
above the village and fill the distant horizon. This is
the heart of the Parque Natural Sierra de Grazalema
(► 21). In the charming Plaza de Andalucía is the
church of Nuestra Señora de la Aurora.

🚻 B3 ✉ 20km west of Ronda 🛈 Plaza de España ☎ 956 13 22
25 🍴 Cádiz El Chico, Plaza de España (€€) 🚌 Daily,
Ronda–Grazalema ♿ Few ❓ Feria de Grazalema 22–25 Aug

SORBAS

Sorbas is the village of the *casas colgadas*, the 'hanging
houses', a picturesque term that sums up its dramatic
clifftop location above a dry valley. There is a strong
tradition of pottery-making: the main workshops are in
the Barrio Alfarero. The central square, the Plaza de la
Constitución, is flanked by the church of Santa María.
The village lies at the heart of the Parque Natural de
Karst en Yesos, a dramatic limestone landscape.

🚻 D3 ✉ 40km northeast of Almería 🍴 Café Bar Teide III, Calle San
Andrés 1 (€) 🚌 Daily, Almería–Sorbas 🛈 Santa Terraplen 9 ☎ 950
36 44 76 ♿ Few ❓ Fiesta Cruz de Mayo, 1–3 May. Fiesta San
Roque, 14–17 Aug

VEJER DE LA FRONTERA

More than most Andalucían Moorish towns and
villages, Vejer is where you come close to the haunting
memory of *Arabic al-Andalus*. The symbol of the
woman wearing the *cobija*, the dark veiling cloak of the
Moors, remains as a token of Vejer's remote hilltop
location and its enchanting maze of narrow streets.

🚻 A3 ✉ 42km southeast of Cádiz 🍴 Bars, cafés and restaurants
(€–€€) 🚌 Daily, Málaga–Cádiz, Cádiz–Vejer. Cádiz buses go to Vejer;
Málaga–Cádiz buses stop on main road below village. From here, 4km
steep walk ♿ Few ❓ Easter Sun, bull-running. Fiestas de la Virgen

VÉLEZ BLANCO

The dramatically situated
village of Vélez Blanco, in the
Sierra María, is difficult to
reach without your own
transport. Its Renaissance
castle seems to grow naturally
from its rocky pinnacle,
opposite the Sphinx-like
mountain butte of La Muela.
The castle is an extension of
an original Moorish Alcazaba,
and dates from the 16th
century. Its sumptuous
interiors were dismantled
wholesale in 1904 after being
sold to a dealer, and now
languish in New York's
Metropolitan Museum, but the
castle still rewards a visit for
its fine views, and the village is
a delightful maze of streets
with balconied houses and
overhanging tiles. A short
distance south are the Cuevas
de los Letreros, where there
are prehistoric cave paintings.

🚻 D2 ✉ 30km north of
Almería 🍴 Bar Sociedad (€)
♿ None

*San Pedro church rising
out from the streets of
Arcos de la Frontera*

53

Museums

MUSEO ARQUEOLÓGICO, GRANADA

Granada's Archaeological Museum is within a
Renaissance palace – the Casa de Castril. The building
has a central patio from whose upper balcony you can
see the Alhambra across a frieze of tiled roofs. A wide
range of exhibits covers the prehistoric, Phoenician,
Roman, Visigothic and Moorish periods and is made
even more impressive by the elegant surroundings.
➕ C3 ✉ Carrera del Darro 43, Granada ☎ 958 22 56 40 ⏱ Tue
3–8, Wed–Sat 9–8, Sun 9–2.30 🚌 Alhambrabus ♿ Few
💷 Inexpensive; free with EU passport

MUSEO ARQUEOLÓGICO PROVINCIAL

Córdoba's Museo Arqueódico Provincial
(Archaeological Museum) occupies a delightful
Renaissance mansion, the Palacio de los Páez. The
arcaded entrance patio, along with the building's
overall charm, its coffered ceilings and elegant
staircases, enhances the excellent displays of
prehistoric, Roman and Moorish exhibits. These
include Roman mosaics and tombstones, and a subtle
Moorish bronze in the form of a stag.
➕ C1 ✉ Plaza Jerónimo Páez, Córdoba ☎ 957 35 55 17 ⏱ Tue
2.30–8.30, Wed–Sat 9–8.30, Sun 9–2.30 🍴 Several cafés (€–€€€)
♿ Few 💷 Inexpensive/free

*The Museo de Artes y
Traditiones, Málaga,
surrounds a peaceful
leafy courtyard*

MUSEO DE ARTES Y TRADITIONES

This excellent museum is located in a restored 17th-
century inn, the Mesón de la Victoria, built round a
little courtyard. On display is a host of traditional
artefacts from the rural and seagoing life of old Málaga
province, a rich reminder of a less frenetic age.
➕ C3 ✉ Calle Pasillo de Santa Isabel 10, Málaga ☎ 952 21 71 37
⏱ Mon–Fri 10–1, 4–7. Closed Sun and public hols 🍴 El Corte Inglés
Buffet Grill (€), Avenida de Andalucía ♿ Few 💷 Inexpensive

MUSEO DEL BELLAS ARTES

The Museo del Bellas Artes is one of Spain's major art
galleries. Located in a beautiful old convent, it
contains 14 rooms displaying superb paintings and
sculpture. Highlights are works by Zurbarán and
Murillo, including the latter's *Virgin and Child*, the
famous '*La Servilleta*', so named because the 'canvas' is
said to be a dinner napkin. There are other works by
Goya, Velázquez and El Greco. Room 5 is dazzling; its
painted roof and Murillo collection are unforgettable.
➕ B2 ✉ Plaza del Museo 9, Seville ☎ 954 78 65 00 ⏱ Tue
2.30–8.30, Wed–Sat 9–8.30, Sun 9–2.30 🍴 El Patio, San Eloy 9 (€–€€)
🚌 C1, C2, C3, C4, C5, 6, 43 ♿ Few 💷 Inexpensive; free with EU passport

Beaches & Resorts

COSTA DEL SOL

Conspicuous tourism is the business of the Costa del Sol, the long ribbon of holiday development that runs from Nerja, east of Málaga, along its western shore to Manilva. Main resorts such as Marbella and Puerto Banús have an upmarket image to match prices, while the middle-range resorts of Torremolinos, Fuengirola, Benalmádena Costa and Estepona cover a range of styles from 'outgoing' to 'retiring'. Smaller resorts, such as Sotogrande and San Pedro de Alcántara, now merge with the seamless concrete of the Costa.

➕ B3 ✉ Between Málaga and Gibraltar 🍴 Enormous number of bars, cafés and restaurants (€–€€€) 🚌 Regular service from Málaga to all resorts 🚆 Regular service Málaga–Torremolinos–Fuengirola

MOJÁCAR

There are two Mojácars, and both are busy places. The old hilltop town of Mojácar Pueblo is hugely popular with the large number of visitors to Mojácar Playa, the straggling beachside development that dominates the nearby coast for several kilometres. Old Mojácar can still charm, in spite of the pressure from relentless summer crowds. After all this, the long narrow beaches of Mojácar Playa are easily reached.

➕ D3 ✉ 65km northeast of Almería 🍴 Numerous bars, cafés, restaurants (€–€€) 🚌 Daily, Almería–Mojácar 🛈 Plaza Nueva ☎ 950 61 50 25 ♿ Few ❓ Moors and Christian Fiesta, 10 Jun. Fiestas Patronales San Augustín, 25–30 Aug

NERJA

Nerja is an enjoyable though busy resort with pleasant beaches, famed for its Balcón de Europa, a palm-lined promontory on the old belvedere of an original fortress. There is an appealing freshness about Nerja, but the form of the old town survives in its narrow streets. It can be crowded, especially at weekends, but it maintains a relaxed air. The best beaches, Calahonda and Burriana, lie to the east of the Balcón.

➕ C3 ✉ 52km east of Málaga 🛈 Puerta del Mar 4 ☎ 952 52 15 31 🍴 Several cafés and restaurants (€–€€€) 🚌 Daily, Málaga—Nerja, Almería–Nerja ♿ Few ❓ Carnival, Feb. Cruces de Mayo, 3 May. Virgen del Carmen, 16 Jul

TARIFA

Tarifa is Europe's most southerly point. Africa is within reach: the blurred outlines of the Moroccan mountains loom across the Strait of Gibraltar only 14km away. Head west from Tarifa to some of the finest, if often breeziest, beaches around.

➕ B3 ✉ 90km southeast of Cádiz 🛈 Paseo de la Alameda s/n ☎ 956 68 09 93; www.tarifaweb.com 🍴 Numerous bars, cafés and restaurants (€–€€€) 🚌 Daily, Málaga–Tarifa, Cádiz–Tarifa ♿ Few ❓ Fiesta de la Virgen de la Luz, 6–13 Sep

COSTA TROPICAL

The Costa Tropical is the westward extension of the Costa de Almería, and occupies Granada province's Mediterranean shoreline. It is less developed than its neighbour and has a stretch of spectacular rocky coastline, a number of pleasant beaches and attractive resorts such as Almuñécar and Salobreña. Almuñécar has some fine Phoenician, Roman and Moorish monuments. The resort's beaches are pebbly and cramped, but the stylish esplanade of Paseo Puerta del Mar makes up for this.

➕ C3 ✉ Adra to Almuñécar 🍴 Numerous bars, cafés and restaurants in various towns and resorts (€–€€€) 🚌 Daily Almería–Málaga ♿ Few

Tarifa harbour

Places to Take the Children

FUN AND GAMES

The Costa del Sol is for fun and games. There are a number of water parks to complement the Costa's numerous beaches and here adults can relax as much as youngsters do. The sheer pace of life on the Costa del Sol, its shops, cafés and restaurants, the crowds and the numerous attractions, are all diverting for youngsters, but inland Andalucía has other attractions. Horse riding is an excellent activity for all the family. Above all, you should find out if there is a festival near you. Spanish children play a major part in such events and children on holiday will be fascinated by it all.

Children love dressing up in traditional costumes at festival time

AQUALAND

A major site with scores of popular water-based attractions, including huge slides, flumes, artificial river, artificial waves, pools, Jacuzzi and much more.
➕ B3 ✉ Calle Cuba 10, Torremolinos ☎ 952 11 49 96/38 88 88; www.aqualand.es 🕐 May–Oct daily 10–6 🍴 Café/restaurant (€€) 🚌 Direct service from Benalmádena Costa Jul–Aug ♿ Few 💶 Expensive

CROCODILE PARK

There are crocodiles large and small to keep everyone amazed. Watch them being fed, at a safe distance, handle cuddly baby alligators and visit the 'Africa' museum.
➕ B3 ✉ Calle Cuba 14, Torremolinos ☎ 952 05 17 82; www.crocodile-park.com 🕐 Mar–Jun, Oct, Nov 10–6; Jul–Sep 10–5 ♿ Poor 💶 Moderate

OASYS

Near Tabernas on the A370, this is the desert hills location for Sergio Leone's famous 'Spaghetti Western' *A Fistful of Dollars*, and for subsequent, similar films. It's now a full-blooded Western theme park, with the old sets convincingly realistic, until you peep behind the façades. Tombstone Gulch saloon is substantially real – there are staged gunfights at High Noon, and a second shift at 5pm. Extra gunfight at 8pm from mid-June to mid-September. There is also a safari wild animal park, the Reserva Zoologica near by.
➕ D3 ✉ Carretera Nacional 340-km, Almería ☎ 950 36 52 36, www.oasyparquetematico.es; 950 36 29 31 (Reserva Zoologica)

PARQUE ACUÁTICO MIJAS

Very wet. A big water fun park with endless pools, slides and flumes. Also on site is 'Aqualandia', a water play area for small children. Also mini-golf and self-service cafeteria, deposit boxes for valuables, and picnic area. Sunbeds, air mattresses and floats for hire. For obvious reasons, there is a strict warning not to bring any form of glass object into the park.
➕ B3 ✉ Circunvalación, Km 290, Mijas Costa ☎ 952 46 04 04/08/09; www.aquamijas.com 🕐 May daily 10.30–5.30; Jun 10–6; Jul–Aug 10–7; Sep–Oct 3 10–6 🍴 Cafetería (€€) 🚌 Direct from Fuengirola bus terminal ♿ Few 💶 Expensive

PARQUE DE LAS CIENCIAS (SCIENCE PARK)

Great fun as well as being informative, the Science Park has numerous hands-on features and ingenious interactive experiences. There is an observatory and planetarium to add to the interest.
➕ C3 ✉ Avenida del Mediterráneo s/n, Granada ☎ 958 13 19 00; www.parqueciencias.com 🕐 Tue–Sat 10–7, Sun 10–3 🚌 5 ♿ Good 💶 Moderate

PARQUE ZOOLOGICO (BOTANICAL GARDENS AND ZOO)

A pleasant facility with a good record of environmentalism and preservation. Various wild animals, many of which are cared for after being injured. The gardens are delightful.

➕ A2 ✉ Calle Taxdirt s/n, Jerez ☎ 956 15 31 64 🕐 Tue–Sun 10–6 🚌 9 ♿ Fair 💰 Moderate

SEA LIFE

A submarine view of Mediterranean sea life from tiny shrimps and shellfish to sharks. Various organised presentations and the feeding displays are popular.

➕ B3 ✉ Puerto Marina, Benalmádena ☎ 952 56 01 50; www.sealifeeurope.com 🕐 Daily 10–6 🍴 Restaurants (€€) 🚆 RENFE Benalmádena ♿ Good 💰 Moderate

SELWO AVENTURA

A magnificent wild animal park covering 100ha where you can see such animals as lions and elephants in their natural habitat.

➕ B3 ✉ Autovia Costa del Sol, Km 162.5, Las Lomas del Monte, Estepona ☎ 902 19 04 82; www.selwo.es 🕐 Mon–Fri 10–6, Sun 10–7.30 ♿ Few 💰 Expensive

TIVOLI WORLD

Funfair rides galore, water flume, Wild West town, open-air theatre, mock Spanish 'plaza', live entertainment. Over a dozen cafés and restaurants cater for all tastes. Very popular during the summer season and busy at weekends, especially.

➕ B3 ✉ Avenida del Tivoli, Arroyo de la Miel, Benalmádena ☎ 952 57 70 16; www.tivoli.es 🕐 Apr, May, 15–30 Sep, Oct 4pm–1am; Jun, 1–14 Sep 5pm–2am; Jul, Aug 6pm–3am; Nov–Mar 11am–9pm 🍴 Numerous cafés and restaurants (€–€€) 🚆 RENFE Benalmádena Arroyo de la Miel ♿ Few 💰 Moderate

WHALES AND DOLPHINS AND WHALE WATCH

Whale- and dolphin-spotting from boats in the Strait of Gibraltar – an exciting day out even though a glimspe of these creatures is not guaranteed. Companies running these include:

FIRMM

➕ B3 ✉ Calle Pedro Cortés 4, Tarifa ☎ 956 62 70 08; www.firmm.org

WHALE WATCH TARIFA

➕ B3 ✉ Avenida de la Constitución 6, Tarifa ☎ 956 62 70 13; www.whalewatchtarifa.net 💰 Expensive

ZOO FUENGIROLA

Magnificent zoo where numerous species of animals and birds can be seen in their natural habitat.

➕ B3 ✉ Camilo José Cela, Fuengirola ☎ 952 66 63 01; www.zoofuengirola.com 🕐 Daily 10–6 (Jul, Aug until 12am) 💰 Moderate

HORSE LOVERS

Yeguada de la Cartuja Hierra del Bocado Stud is a paradise for horse-mad youngsters – and for everyone, in fact. Thoroughbred horses are carefully bred and raised as this state-owned stud. Open days enable visitors to see the horses in action, drawing carriages and going through training. Reservations are advised and can be made by phone or through hotels.

➕ A2 ✉ Finca Fuente El Suero, Carretera Medina-El Portal 6.5 km, Jerez ☎ 956 16 28 09; www.yeguadacartuja.com 🕐 Sat only, 11am 💰 Expensive

Activities

Windsurfing conditions are perfect on the Costa de la Luz

BIRDWATCHING
In spite of widespread shooting and other hazards, birds flock in and out of coastal Andalucía, especially in spring and autumn. The coastal nature parks are the places to be.

FOOTBALL MATCH
If there is a big match on, especially somewhere like Málaga, go along for the fantastic atmosphere.

HORSERIDING
In the land of great horse-handling and riding, what else should you do?

MOUNTAIN BIKING
The Sierra Nevada has become one of the leading mountain biking destinations in Europe. Several British-founded companies offer guided tours.

PEOPLE-WATCHING
The ultimate activity. Choose a good café in a busy plaza or village square, morning or evening.

SCUBA-DIVING
Andalucía under water can be as spectacular as it can be on land.

SIGHTSEEING
Everywhere, you will be spoiled for choice.

SWIMMING
The entire coast of Andalucía is yours to choose from, but look out for village and local swimming pools deep inland. They can be real life savers.

TENNIS AND GOLF
The Costa del Sol is the place for these sports. There are numerous courts and courses, although you may need to book well ahead and join a queue.

WALKING
This is a rather non-Andalucían habit. But in the mountains, or along the more remote coastline, it is a glorious way of enjoying the country.

WINDSURFING
Head for the Tarifa coastline of the Costa de la Luz for some of the best windsurfing conditions in the world.

WINE-TASTING
Visit the bodegas of Jerez de la Frontera for an eye-opening insight into the complex world of sherry. Tours include tastings and even visits to vineyards.

Historic Sites

---- **In the Top 25** ----
🟥 **REALES ALCÁZARES, SEVILLE (► 44)**

BAÑOS ÁRABES

On the way along the Carrera del Darro from Plaza Nueva are the Baños Árabes (Arab Baths), a small but enchanting Moorish bathhouse, entered through a tiny courtyard garden with inlaid floor and tiny central pool. The 11th-century baths are well preserved and have the typical star-shape and octagon-shape skylights in the roofs of their brick-vaulted chambers.

➕ C3 ✉ Northeast of Plaza Nueva, Granada ☎ 958 02 78 00
🍴 Numerous bars and restaurants (€–€€) 🚍 Alhambrabus ♿ Few

CASA NATAL DE PICASSO

You cannot fault a city whose most famous son was one of the world's greatest painters, Pablo Ruiz y Picasso (1881–1973). The Casa Natal Picasso (Picasso's Birthplace) is the headquarters of the Picasso Foundation, and is located in a handsome terrace of 19th-century houses in the large and friendly Plaza de la Merced, with its big central memorial. The building is significant more for its sense of Picasso's presence than for its rather spare (though elegant) rooms, converted out of Picasso's early home. There are some fine mementoes and photographs of the artist, not least the striking photograph in the entrance foyer.

➕ C3 ✉ Plaza de la Merced 15, Málaga
☎ 952 06 02 15 🕐 Daily 9.30–8
🍴 Several cafés in Plaza de la Merced (€)
♿ Few 🎫 Free

CASTILLO DE GIBRALFARO

The much-renovated Moorish Castillo de Gibralfaro (Castle of Gibralfaro) stands high above Málaga and above the Alcazaba, to which it is connected by a parapet wall. There are exhilarating views from the ramparts and from the terraced approach path, that leads you up from the Alcazaba amid a deluge of bougainvillea and flower beds – but hang on to your wallet or handbag.

➕ C3 ✉ Monte del Faro, Málaga
☎ 952 22 72 30 🕐 Daily 9–6 (summer until 7.45) 🍴 Parador de Málaga Gibralfaro (€€€) 🚍 35 from Paseo del Parque.
Horse–drawn carriages also make the trip from the Paseo del Parque and from outside the cathedral ♿ Few 🎫 Inexpensive

ITÁLICA

The Roman ruins of Itálica lie 9km north of Seville and can be reached by regular bus from the city's Plaza de Arma bus station. Itálica is remarkable, not least for its amphitheatre and for the ruins of its Roman city.

➕ B2 ✉ Santiponce ☎ 955 99 65 83 🕐 Closed Mon and festivals 🎫 Inexpensive; free with EU passport

Baños Árabes, Granada

Places to Have Lunch

Relaxing beneath the sunshades after lunch

AR GIRALDA (€–€€)
For a memorable lunch stop, come to one of the best *tapas* bars in Seville.
🔲 B2 ✉ Mateos Gago 1, Seville ☎ 954 22 74 35

EL CHINITAS (€)
Popular *tapas* bar and traditional restaurant offering regional specialities.
🔲 C3 ✉ Calle Moreno Monroy 4–6, Málaga ☎ 952 21 09 72

GAITÁN (€€)
Contender for the most popular restaurant in town, with a good reputation for quality cooking. *Rabo de toro a la Jerezana* (bull's tail Jerez-style) features as one of its specialities.
🔲 A2 ✉ Gaitán 3, Jerez ☎ 956 16 80 21

MESON DIEGO (€)
An atmospheric local bar-restaurant where you can sit outside, eat good food and get a taste of Andalucían life.
🔲 C3 ✉ Plaza Constitución 12, Alhama de Granada ☎ 958 36 01 21

EL MOLINO (€–€€)
Pleasant terrace overlooking Ronda's busiest square. Choose from the good selection of main dishes and desserts.
🔲 B3 ✉ Plaza del Socorro 6, Ronda ☎ 952 87 93 32

LA PARRALA (€)
Charming situation on the gleaming white Plaza de las Monjas, alongside the walls of the Convento de Santa Clara. A popular gathering place for locals in the evenings.
🔲 A2 ✉ Plaza de las Monjas 22, Moguer ☎ 959 37 04 52

EL PORTALON (€€€)
One of the coast's top-notch restaurants, with an excellent selection of fresh seafood dishes and roast meats.
🔲 A3 ✉ Carretera Cádiz, Km 178 ☎ 952 86 10 75

SIENA (€)
Well-placed café-restaurant for watching the world go by in the attractive Plaza de las Tendillas. Drinks, snacks and *platas combinados*.
🔲 C1 ✉ Plaza de las Tendillas, Córdoba ☎ 957 47 30 05

VIA COLÓN (€€)
This charming place near the cathedral has a pleasant outside terrace and serves tasty snacks and local specialities.
🔲 C3 ✉ Gran Via de Colón 13, Granada ☎ 958 22 98 42

ANDALUCÍA
where to...

Córdoba & Jaén

TAPAS

The *tapa* takes the form of a snack or titbit that can range from a few olives or a sliver of *jamón serrano* (dried ham) on oil-soaked bread to more elaborate mixtures of fish, meat, cheese and vegetables. The word *tapa* means 'lid' and the *tapa* tradition may have derived from the habit of covering drinks with a small dish or a slice of bread to protect them from insects and dust. The *tapeo*, an evening jaunt round the bars enjoying *tapas*, ideally accompanied by chilled *fino* sherry or beer, (never by coffee), is now enshrined in the food lore of Andalucía. Most *tapas* that include tuna fish, *atún*, are fairly certain to be tasty. Try *redondillos de atún*, if you come across it. This is tuna mixed with eggs and breadcrumbs and cooked in a white wine sauce.

BAEZA

CASA JUANITO (€€)

Tasty and unusual dishes based on traditional recipes. Specialities include partridge salad, fillet of beef with tomatoes and peppers, and artichoke hearts with tomatoes and garlic. In the hotel of the same name.
✉ Avenida Arca del Agua
☎ 953 74 00 40 🕐 Lunch and dinner. Closed dinner Sun and Mon

LA GÓNDOLA (€)

Cosy bar and restaurant with brick and tile interior and open fireplace. *Tapas* include the tasty speciality *patatas baezanas*, sautéed potatoes topped with fried mushrooms, parsley and garlic.
✉ Portales Carboneria 13
☎ 953 74 29 84 🕐 Lunch and dinner

CAZORLA

CAFÉ DE LA CARREDERA (€)

This café in Cazorla's new square also has a tempting range of international beers. You can relax here most times of the day, early to late.
✉ Plaza de la Corredera
☎ 953 72 01 02
🕐 Breakfast, lunch and dinner

LA SARGA (€€€)

Cazorla's most refined dining experience comes in the unlikely form of La Sarga, a restaurant where chef José Polaina transforms rustic meals for mountain people into rustic meals for fine diners. Regardless, the wine list has a fantastic selection of local wines.
✉ Plaza del Mercado 2
☎ 953 72 15 07;
www.lasarga.com 🕐 Wed–Mon lunch and dinner

CÓRDOBA

EL CABALLO ROJO (€€–€€€)

Excellent Córdoban cuisine at this famous restaurant near the Mezquita, frequented by royalty when they're in town. Specialises in local dishes, such as partridge breasts, lamb and honey and *rabo de toro* (oxtail).
✉ Cardenal Herrero 28 ☎ 957 47 53 75 🕐 Lunch and dinner

LOS CALIFAS (€€)

Attractive restaurant in the old quarter, with a pleasant rooftop terrace. Specialises in Córdoban regional cuisine, with good meat specialities.
✉ Calle Deanes 3 ☎ 957 47 13 20 🕐 Lunch and dinner

EL CHURRASCO (€€)

Top-quality restaurant whose staff and management are rather well aware of the fact. Andalucían cuisine at its finest, with dishes such as *gaspacho de habas*, delicious cold soup made from broad beans and spiced with almonds and other delicacies. Top end of price range for special dishes, but with a reasonable set menu.
✉ Calle Romero 16 ☎ 957 29 08 19 🕐 Lunch and dinner. Closed Aug

PIZZAIOLO (€)

Well-run pizzeria in an attractive square, with a good selection of tasty,

if predictable food.
Features, proudly, in
Guinness Book of Records
as having 360 different
selections.

✉ Calle San Felipe 5 ☎ 957
48 64 33 ⏰ Lunch and dinner

TABERNA SAN MIGUEL (€)

One of Córdoba's most
popular establishments,
with a lively ambience
and a wide selection of
tapas.

✉ Plaza San Miguel 1 ☎ 957
47 83 28 ⏰ Lunch and dinner

JAÉN

CASA VICENTE (€€€)

Top Jaén eating place,
housed in a restored
palace near the cathedral.
Excellent local cuisine
with game specialities.

✉ Calle Francisco Marín Mora 1
☎ 953 23 22 22 ⏰ Lunch
and dinner. Closed Sun dinner and
Aug

PARADOR DE JAÉN (€€)

High-quality cuisine in
high surroundings at the
restaurant of Jaén's
Moorish *parador*.
Andalucían specialities
such as the famous
morcilla en caldera (blood
sausage), served in mock-
medieval surroundings.
Reservations advised for
non-residents.

✉ Castillo de Santa Catalina
☎ 953 23 00 00 ⏰ Lunch
and dinner

PROIEGO DE CÓRDOBA

LA NORIA

Enjoying one of the best
locations in town, the
sunny side of the Abad

Palomino square, La
Noria is a great spot for a
light lunch or drink. The
menu ranges from light
salads to roasted pork and
other local dishes.

✉ Abad Palomino 18 ☎ 957
54 27 27; www.epriego.com/
lanoria ⏰ Lunch and dinner

ÚBEDA

EL GALLO ROJO (€)

Good value options at
this popular restaurant
to the north of Plaza de
Andalucía, a reasonable
distance from a busy
junction. Reservations
advised. Regional dishes
can be enjoyed at outside
tables.

✉ Calle Manuel Barraca 3
☎ 953 75 20 38 ⏰ Lunch
and dinner

MESON BARBACOA (€)

Intriguing restaurant-cum-
agricultural museum. The
walls are crammed with
farming implements and
the rafters hung with
traditional bags, baskets
and containers. Good
selection of *platos
combinados* to go with it.

✉ Calle San Cristobal 17
☎ 953 79 04 73
⏰ Lunch and dinner

ZUHEROS

RESTAURANT ZUHAYRA (€€)

In the hotel of the same
name and with a good
selection of local dishes,
often flavoured with the
area's famous olive oil.
Córdoba province's equally
famous *montilla* wine
should be compulsory.

✉ Calle Mirador 10 ☎ 957 69
46 93 ⏰ Lunch and dinner

PINCHO, RACIÓN AND PLATO COMBINADO

The smallest *tapa* is often
referred to as a *pincho*. More
substantial helpings of *tapas*
are called *raciónes* and are a
meal in themselves. A *ración*
should cost no more than
about €6. A popular option is
a *plato combinado*, a mix of
food with bread and often a
drink. A *plato combinado*
should cost no more than
about €8. Pictures of the
choice of *platos combinados*
available at each restaurant
are often displayed.

63

Granada & Almeria

TABLE CHARGES

In city bars and cafés there are varying charges for the same *tapas* or *raciones*, depending on where you eat. Standing at the bar in time-honoured *tapeo* fashion will cost the least. Eating at a table will cost more, and eating outside on the pavement or 'terrace' may cost more again. If you eat at the bar, pay at the bar. If you want to sit at a table, whether inside or outside, expect waiter service.

ALHAMA DE LA GRANADA

MESON DIEGO (€)
Good local café-restaurant where you may even enjoy free *tapas* with your drinks before ordering a sit-down meal at the broad terrace, usually in the company of local people, alongside Alhama's pleasant central square.
⊠ Plaza Constitucion 12
☎ 958 36 01 21 🕓 Lunch and dinner

ALMERIA

ASADOR TORRELUZ (€€)
Part of the Torreluz Hotel complex on Almería's charming Plaza Flores, this top-class restaurant is renowned for its local and international cuisine.
⊠ Plaza Flores 1 ☎ 950 23 49 99 🕓 Lunch and dinner. Closed Sun

EL BELLO RINCÓN (€€)
Considered to be one of Almería's top restaurants, offering fine sea views and excellent fresh seafood.
⊠ Carretera Nacional 340 Km 436 ☎ 950 23 84 27 🕓 Lunch only. Closed Mon, Jul and Aug

BODEGA LAS BOTAS (€€)
Well aware of its appeal, this delightful *tapas* bar is still irresistible. Try and sit at the barrel tables if you're sampling wine – and there's plenty of choice – or at the neat little tables on the other side of the bar for *jámon* and fish dishes at their best.
⊠ Calle Fructuoso Pérez 3
☎ No phone 🕓 Dinner

BUBIÓN

LA ARTESA RESTAURANTE (€€)
Attractive small bar and restaurant specialising in roast leg of pork and *choto al ajillo* (kid cooked with garlic). Andalucían dark wood and bright tilework.
⊠ Carretera de la Sierra 2
☎ 958 76 34 37 🕓 Lunch and dinner. Closed Mon and Sun evening

CAPILEIRA

POQUEIRA (€)
Good little restaurant attached to the hotel of the same name. Local dishes at their best and reasonably priced.
⊠ Calle Doctor Castilla 6
☎ 958 76 30 48 🕓 Lunch and dinner. Closed Mon

GRANADA

CARMEN VERDE LUNA (€€–€€€)
Trading on its unbeatable views of the Alhambra, this terrace restaurant in the Albaicin, close to the Mirador de San Nicolás, serves modern Andalucían cuisine.
⊠ Camino Nuevo de San Nicolás 16 ☎ 958 29 17 94 🕓 Lunch and dinner, later in summer

CHIKITO (€€)
Popular 'literary' eating place once patronised by García Lorca and by English writers on the romantic Andalucían trail. Just north of the Carrera del Genil promenade in a leafy square. Expensive international dishes, but with a reasonably priced set menu.

✉ Plaza del Campillo 9
☎ 958 22 33 64 🕐 Lunch
and dinner. Closed Wed

**MESON EL TRILLO
(€–€€)**
Rustic home-cooking
is the speciality of this
delightful, small
restaurant in the Albaicín.
There's a patio with
shaded seating and a cosy
interior for the winter
months.
✉ Callejón del Aljibe del Trillo
☎ 958 22 51 82 🕐 Lunch
and dinner

**MIRADOR DE
MORAYMA (€€)**
Housed in a handsome
16th-century mansion in
the old quarter of
Albaicín, this restaurant
has good cuisine. The
delightful leafy terrace has
magnificent views over
the Alhambra.
✉ Pianista García Carillo 2,
Albaicín ☎ 958 22 82 90
🕐 Lunch and dinner. Closed Sun

NUEVO (€)
The row of tables beside
the marble bar is always
filled with locals. There's
a variety of set menus that
are exceptionally good
value – it won't win
awards but it is a bargain.
✉ 25 Calle Navas ☎ 958 22
67 63 🕐 Lunch and dinner

SEVILLA (€€)
This venerable Granadine
restaurant located at the
heart of the cathedral area
offers a reasonably priced
menu. There's also a good
tapas bar, and a pleasant
outside seating area.
✉ Officios 12 ☎ 958 22 12
23 🕐 Lunch and dinner. Closed
Sun evenings and Mon

SAN NICOLÁS (€€€)
A striking restaurant with
columns and chandeliers.
Choose a table by the
window for great views of
the Alhambra. The menu
includes such nouvelle-
Andaluz dishes as leg of
pork filled with lavender
and honey.
✉ Calle San Nicolás 3 ☎ 958
80 42 62 🕐 Lunch and dinner.
Closed Wed

GUADIX

COMERCIO (€€)
A top-quality restaurant
located in the hotel of the
same name. It has won
several awards for its
cooking; the local and
international dishes come
highly recommended.
✉ Calle Mira de Amezcua 3
☎ 958 66 05 00 🕐 Lunch
and dinner

MOJÁCAR

**PARADOR DE
MOJÁCAR (€€€)**
Fine local cuisine in this
modern restaurant, part of
the Mojácar *parador*. Try
gambones de Gaurruchera, a
tasty prawn dish. Delicious
desserts. Reservations
advised for non-residents.
✉ Playa de Mojácar s/n
☎ 950 47 82 50 🕐 Lunch
and dinner

VELÉZ BLANCO

MESÓN EL MOLINO (€€)
A relaxed eating place
tucked away in a narrow
alley off the main street
with a good range of
regional dishes.
✉ Plaza Curtidores 1 ☎ 950
41 50 70 🕐 Lunch and dinner.
Closed Thu, Sun evening and Jul

BREAKFAST

Breakfast (*desayuno*) can be
had at local bars and cafés by
8am and even earlier, but for
most visitors, breakfast at
about 10am is usual and is at
its most enjoyable when taken
on a café terrace, in the shade.
Orange juice is the genuine
article, and is delicious. You
can follow this with *tostadas*,
big slices of roll which can be
doused with olive oil from
metal jugs or spread with
butter and then jam
(*mermelada*). Coffee is always
available, but if you want tea,
do not ask for tea with milk (*té
con leche*). Make it clear that
you want the tea black, and
that milk should be brought to
you separately; otherwise you
might end up with a soggy tea
bag drowning in boiled milk.
Chocolate y churros (hot
chocolate and spiral-shaped
doughnuts) are another
popular option for breakfast,
especially during the winter
months. There's really no such
thing as a breakfast *tapas*, but
if you want something other
than *tostadas* and
mermelada, try a slice of
tortilla española (potato
omelette) or *jamón serrano*
and *huevo cocido* (cured ham
and boiled egg).

Málaga & Cádiz

ANTEQUERA

EL ANGELOTE (€€)
Centrally located across
from the museum, this
excellent restaurant serves
fine local cuisine. Try the
setas (oyster mushrooms)
with garlic and rosemary,
or wild partridge. The
desserts are delicious, and
more varied than the ice-
cream and *flan* norm.
✉ Calle Encarnación (corner
Coso Viejo) ☎ 952 70 34 65
🕐 Lunch and dinner. Closed Mon

ARCOS DE LA FRONTERA

EL CONVENTO (€€)
Pleasant restaurant of
hotel of same name, at
the heart of the old town.
Outstanding traditional
cuisine with game dishes a
speciality. You pay less for
the set menu, but this is
still quite expensive.
✉ Calle Maldonado 2 ☎ 956
70 32 32 🕐 Lunch and dinner.
Closed 17–22 Jan

CÁDIZ

BALANDRO (€)
A local favourite, with a
pleasant terrace as well as
an inside dining area
Excellent Cádiz fish and
seafood *tapas*, and *raciones*.
✉ Alameda Apodaca 22
☎ 956 22 09 92 🕐 Lunch
and dinner

EL FARO (€€)
Rated as one of the best
fish restaurants around.
The paella is excellent, as
are the great local dishes
featuring bream, octopus
and hake.
✉ Calle San Felix 15 ☎ 956
22 99 16 🕐 Lunch and dinner

**MESÓN CUMBRES
MAYORES (€–€€)**
Good lively *tapas* bar and
restaurant. A great variety
of dishes include fish,
seafood and barbecued
meats.
✉ Calle Zorilla ☎ 956 21 32
70 🕐 Lunch and dinner

GIBRALTAR

LA BAYUCA (€€€)
One of the oldest
restaurants on the Rock,
well known for its
Mediterranean specialities
with an extensive menu
and emphasis on seafood.
Delicious desserts and
swift, friendly service.
✉ 21 Turnbull Lane ☎ 350 77
51 19 🕐 Lunch and dinner.
Closed Sun lunch and Tue

JEREZ

EL GALLO AZUL (€)
Central *tapas* bar with a
high turnover and some
award-winning *tapas*,
making it a good bet when
other bars are closed or
crowded.
✉ Calle Large 2 ☎ 956 32 61
48; www.casajuancarlos.com
🕐 Lunch and dinner until late

GAITÁN (€€)
A prize-winning restaurant
that offers good value
traditional and nouvelle
cuisine, with fish dishes a
speciality.
✉ Calle Gaitán 3 ☎ 956 16
80 21; www.restaurantegaitan.
com 🕐 Lunch and dinner

MÁLAGA

BAR LO GÜENO (€)
One of the best-known
tapas bars in Málaga, with
more than 75 varieties

to choose from. The L-shaped bar is very cramped, but there are tables outside. Excellent range of Rioja wines.

✉ Calle Marín García 9 ☎ No phone 🕒 Lunch and dinner. Closed Sun

CASA PEDRO (€–€€)

Long-established, family-run fish restaurant in El Palo. The dining-room overlooks the sea and the seafood is very fresh. If you don't mind the noise and bustle, come here for Sunday lunch, when Malagueño families traditionally dine out

✉ Quitapenas 121, El Palo ☎ 952 29 00 13 🕒 Lunch and dinner. Closed Mon

MARBELLA

SANTIAGO (€€€)

An elegant restaurant with an excellent position right on the seafront. It offers the very best fresh fish and seafood along with an extensive wine list.

✉ Paseo Marítimo 5 ☎ 952 77 43 39 🕒 Lunch and dinner. Closed Nov

MEDINA SIDONIA

BAR CÁDIZ (€)

This centrally located bar-restaurant has a traditional menu and a good selection of tapas.

✉ Plaza España 14 ☎ 956 41 02 50 🕒 Lunch and dinner

NERJA

CASA LUQUE (€€)

One of Nerja's most popular establishments, which is housed in an old Andalucían mansion. The cuisine is from the north of Spain, and can be eaten on the attractive patio open for outdoor dining in summer.

✉ Plaza Cavana 2 ☎ 952 52 10 04 🕒 Lunch and dinner

RONDA

PEDRO ROMERO (€€)

Popular, award-winning restaurant; walls covered in bullfighting photographs. *Rabo de toro a la Rondeña*, Ronda-style bull's-tail stew, is a speciality, or try the grilled salmon.

✉ Virgen de la Paz 18 ☎ 952 87 11 10 🕒 Lunch and dinner

RESTAURANT DON MIGUEL (€€)

Hotel restaurant, with indoor eating and spacious terraces on several levels, offering views of Ronda's gorge.

✉ Plaza de España 4 ☎ 952 87 77 22 🕒 Lunch and dinner

TARIFA

BAR MORILLA (€)

Pleasant *tapas* bar with outside seating, at the very heart of the town. Good local dishes.

✉ Calle Sancho IV El Bravo s/n ☎ 956 68 17 57 🕒 Lunch and dinner

TORREMOLINOS

BODEGA QUITAPENAS (€)

Much favoured by locals and tourists for its reasonably priced *tapas* and seafood dishes, and its position on the steps leading down to the beach.

✉ Calle Cuesta del Tajo 3 🕒 Lunch and dinner

TAPAS TIP

Unless you are fluent in Spanish and don't mind what you eat, be careful about sticking a pin in a typical menu board outside a bar, café or restaurant. A *tapa* can be anything from *chicharrón* (pork scratchings), to *criadillas* (fried testicles of pig), so make sure you know what a *tapa* is describing. Good names to look for in lists of *tapas* are *calamares* (squid), *anchoas* (anchovies), *champiñones* (mushrooms), *chorizo* (spicy sausage) and *jamón serrano* (cured ham). Names that might give you pause for thought, or challenge the adventurous, are *callos* or *menudo* (tripe), *burgajo* or *caracoles* (snails), *sesos* (brains) and the Granada speciality, *tortilla al sacromonte* (omelette made with lambs' testicles and brains). *Tapas* for vegetarians to look out for include *aceitunas* (olives), *habas* (broad beans) *ensaladilla* (salad, often with dressing), *berenjenas con miel* (fried slices of aubergine with honey), *pisto* (vegetable stew), *patatas alí-oli* (fried potatoes in garlic mayonnaise), *huevos revueltos* (scrambled egg) and *queso* (cheese).

Seville & Huelva

TOP RESTAURANTS

The top Andalucían restaurants can match any in Europe for the quality of their cuisine, and you will find international dishes on offer in the best city restaurants. The more formal restaurants often include *Restaurante* or *Mesón* in their titles. Regional dishes are also available, and there are chefs producing new and exciting cuisine with a regional bias. Andalucía, especially in places such as Málaga, Cádiz and Sanlúcar de Barrameda, is famous for its fish dishes. A mainly fish restaurant is called a *marisquería* and, although the very best of these are found on the coast, many inland restaurants offer excellent fish dishes.

ARACENA

CASAS (€€)
Well-run, prize-winning restaurant specialising in traditional Sierra Morena cuisine. Impressive wine list. On the way up to the Gruta de las Maravillas.
✉ Casas Colmenitas 41 ☎ 959 12 82 12 🕒 Lunch and dinner

AYAMONTE

PARADOR DE AYAMONTE (€€€)
Superb restaurant within this magnificent *parador*, with its sweeping views of the river. Try the regional seafood specialities such as *calamar relleno* (stuffed squid) and *raya en pimiento* (stingray with red pepper).
✉ El Castillito (Ayamonte) ☎ 959 32 07 00 🕒 Lunch and dinner

CARMONA

ALCÁZAR DEL REY DON PEDRO (€€€)
Restaurant in Carmona's handsome *parador*, open to non-residents. High-quality cuisine comprising local specialities and international dishes. They include *cartuja de perdiz* (partridge with vegetables). The Carmona can get very busy, so reservations are advised.
✉ Alcázar, s/n ☎ 954 14 10 10 🕒 Lunch and dinner

LA ALMAZARA DE CARMONA (€€)
Moorish décor in a pleasant restaurant on the eastern side of town. There is a good selection of salads and vegetable dishes using fresh local produce. Excellent home-made desserts.
✉ Santa Anna 33 ☎ 954 19 00 76 🕒 Lunch and dinner

ÉCIJA

BODEGON DEL GALLEGO (€€)
Located just round the corner from the Palacio de Peñaflor, this popular and well-run restaurant offers good fish dishes. Pick your own lobster, if you can bear to, from a display tank. Reserve ahead.
✉ Calle Arcipreste Aparicio 3 ☎ 954 83 26 18 🕒 Lunch and dinner

HUELVA

TABERNA EL CONDADO (€)
Lively *tapas* bar in the old part of town. Rustic flavour that is popular with locals.
✉ Calle Sor Ángela de la Cruz 3 ☎ 959 26 11 23 🕒 Lunch and dinner. Closed Sun

MOGUER

MESON EL LOBITO (€)
Fascinating El Lobito is housed in a cavernous building, the walls of which are dense with the graffiti of patrons' names. Cobwebbed and soot-encased oddments hang from the rafters. Alongside the bar is a huge open fire, on which food is grilled.
✉ Calle Rábida 31 ☎ 959 37 06 60 🕒 Lunch and dinner

OSUNA

CASA CURRO (€)
Excellent *tapas* bar and a good standard menu in this

pleasant bar-restaurant in a small attractive square. A local favourite.

✉ Plaza Salitre 5–9 ☎ 955 82 07 58 🕒 Breakfast, lunch and dinner

DOÑA GUADALUPE (€)

Popular restaurant situated on a small square. It has a good reputation for its cuisine and a pleasant patio for outdoor eating.

✉ Plaza Guadalupe 6 ☎ 954 81 05 58 🕒 Lunch and dinner. Closed Tue

SEVILLE

BAR ESTRELLA (€)

This low-key, 70-year-old *tapas* bar has one of the best *tapas* menus in Seville, with delicacies such as *solomillo al whisky* (pork flambéed in Johnnie Walker). You'll find it between the cathedral and Plaza Alfalfa.

✉ Calle Estrella 3 ☎ No phone

CASA ROBLES (€€)

Family-run restaurant dating from the early '50s, a short walk from the cathedral, The *azulejo*-clad walls are typically Andaluz – as is the cuisine, including fish soup and Serrano ham, plus tempting desserts.

✉ Calle Álvarez Quintero 58 ☎ 954 21 31 50 🕒 Lunch and dinner

CORRAL DEL AGUA (€–€€)

Housed in a former 18th-century mansion in the Santa Cruz district, this restaurant features a delightful plant-filled courtyard for dining out in the summer. Andalucían-style dishes.

✉ Callejón del Agua 6 ☎ 954 22 48 41 🕒 Lunch and dinner. Closed Sun, 2 weeks in Feb

LA CUEVA (€€)

Patio restaurant at the heart of the Santa Cruz area. Excellent fish dishes, *paella* and lamb specialities.

✉ Calle Rodrigo Caro 18 ☎ 954 21 31 43 🕒 Lunch and dinner

ENRIQUE BECERRA (€€)

Attractive eatery with an international reputation, between Plaza Nueva and the bullring. Try the *salad de pâte et crabe* (pasta and spider crab salad), or roasted lamb with honey and spinach and pine seed stuffing.

✉ Calle Gamazo 2 ☎ 954 21 30 49 🕒 Lunch and dinner. Closed Sun

EL GIRALDILLO (€€)

Great *tapas* selection in this popular restaurant in sight of Seville's cathedral. Try the eggs 'flamenco style', a subtle mix of eggs, tomatoes, garlic, onions and salami. Excellent gazpacho.

✉ Plaza Virgen de los Reyes 2 ☎ 954 21 45 25 🕒 Lunch and dinner

HOTEL ALFONSO XIII (€€€)

Dining here demands serious money, but the surroundings might just make you feel like a millionaire. Lunch is less of a drain on resources and offers an excellent choice.

✉ Calle San Fernando 2 ☎ 954 91 70 00 🕒 Lunch and dinner

CHOOSING WHAT TO EAT

Restaurants usually offer a fixed-price menu of the day, called *menú del día* or *menú de la casa*. This will usually be a two- or three-course meal with bread and wine and will cost from €10 to €19. Confusingly for North Europeans, a list showing a selection of dishes at a restaurant is called *la carta*, not a *menú*. Ask for *la carta* if you want to make your own selection. A meal from *la carta* costs more than the *menú del día*.

Córdoba & Jaén

PRICES

Prices are approximate for a double room, excluding breakfast and taxes:

€ = under €60
€€ = €60–€150
€€€ = over €150

WHERE TO STAY

The main distinctions between accommodation options in Andalucía are between *fondas*, *pensiones* (pensions), *hostales* (hostels) and *hoteles* (hotels). *Fondas*, with an 'F' sign, and *pensiones*, with a 'P' sign, are inexpensive and can be quite basic, but are often more than adequate and can sometimes supply meals. Hostels, marked with an 'H' sign, are often quite numerous in larger towns and cities. They can also be inexpensive and usually have a mix of en-suite rooms and rooms with a shared bathroom. Standards vary, but some hostels can be excellent value and full of character. The better ones may have air-conditioning. Hotels are graded from one to five stars. Below three stars, there is often little distinction between hotels and hostels. Above three stars, hotels become significantly more expensive and you will find the same facilities and service that you would expect to find in similarly starred hotels throughout Europe.

BAEZA

HOSPEDERÍA FUENTENUEVA (€€)
Charming small hotel, once a prison – now transformed with sophistication. Excellent restaurant.
✉ Avenida Puche Pardo s/n
☎ 953 74 31 00;
www.fuentenueva.com

CAZORLA

HOTEL GUADALQUIVIR (€€)
A pleasant hotel located at the heart of the town between Plaza Corredera and Plaza Santa Maria.
✉ Calle Nueva 6 ☎ 953 72 02 68; www.hguadalquivir.com

CÓRDOBA

HOTEL MEZQUITA (€€)
Conveniently opposite the Mosque. Former 16th-century mansion, restored in typical Spanish style, with a charming courtyard.
✉ Plaza Santa Catalina
☎ 957 47 55 85

HOTEL LOS OMEYAS (€€)
In the heart of the 'Judería', only a few steps from the Mezquita and other attractions. Arab motifs throughout, including a traditional courtyard patio.
✉ Calle Encarnacion 17
☎ 957 49 22 67

JAÉN

HOTEL XAUEN (€€)
Off the Plaza de la Constitución. Rooms have air-conditioning. Self-service coffee shop.
✉ Plaza de Deán Mazas 3
☎ 953 24 07 89;
www.hotelxanenjaen.com

PRIEGO DE CÓRDOBA

HOSTAL RAFI (€)
At the bottom end of the price range, this delightful *hostal* lies in a narrow street near the Plaza de la Constitución.
✉ Isabel la Católica 4 ☎ 957 54 07 49; www.hostalrafi.net

SEGURA DE LA SIERRA

LOS HUERTOS DE SEGURA (€€)
At the village's highest point, with apartments for 2 to 4 people, with bathroom, kitchenette, open fireplace and magnificent views. Welcoming atmosphere.
✉ Calle Castillo 11 ☎ 953 48 04 02; www.loshuertosdesegura.com

ÚBEDA

PARADOR DE ÚBEDA (€€)
Charming spot in the Plaza de Vázquez de Molina. Originally a 16th-century palace, the *parador* retains many period features, such as an inner courtyard with galleries and rooms with high ceilings.
✉ Plaza de Vázquez Molina s/n
☎ 953 75 03 45; www.parador.es

ZUHEROS
HOTEL ZUHAYRA (€€)
Delightful little hotel with its own pool and patio. Tasty local dishes in the restaurant.
✉ Calle Mirador 10 ☎ 957 69 46 93

Granada & Almeria

ALHAMA DE LA GRANADA

BALNEARIO DE ALHAMA DE GRANADA (€€)

Long-established spa hotel built over preserved Moorish baths. The hotel has a plain appearance, which is compensated by its attractive, riverside location among trees. Thermal baths and other health treatments are available.
✉ Carretera del Balneario s/n ☎ 958 35 00 11/03 66; www.balnearioalhamadegranada.com

ALMERÍA

GRAN HOTEL ALMERÍA (€€€)

Luxury hotel located at the seaward end of the Rambla de Belén. Close to the old town, but out of Puerta de Purchena focus, although it makes up for it with its own disco and swimming pool.
✉ Avenida Reina Regente 8 ☎ 950 23 80 11; www.granhotelalmeria.com

HOTEL LA PERLA (€€)

Family-run hotel, said to be the oldest in Almería. Located just off the Puerta Purchena's busy square, the liveliest part of town, but detached enough from too much street noise.
✉ Plaza del Carmen 7 ☎ 950 23 88 77; www.githoteles.com

HOTEL TORRELUZ III/HOTEL TORRELUZ II (€€–€€€)

Two hotels in an attractive square, under the same management. Hotel Torreluz II is the more expensive and stylish. Hotel Torreluz is of the same basic standard, but is in a more anonymous building. Both are associated with excellent restaurants. (There is a third Torreluz hotel in the square. This is AM Torreluz; independent of and more expensive than its namesakes.)
✉ Plaza Flores 3 (Torreluz III); Plaza Flores 6 (Torreluz II) ☎ 950 23 43 99; www.torreluz.com (both hotels)

BÉRCHULES

LA POSADA (€)

Excellent base for exploring Las Alpujarras. Authentic Alpujarras-style house, hundreds of years old, at the heart of Bérchules. Evening meal and breakfast. Local 'house' wine recommended. English spoken by friendly proprietors.
✉ Plaza del Ayuntamiento s/n ☎ 958 85 25 41

BUBIÓN

VILLA TURÍSTICA DE BUBIÓN (€€)

Purpose-built hotel of 43 houses built as replicas of traditional Alpujarran dwellings, all with terrace or private garden.
✉ Barrio Alto s/n ☎ 958 76 39 09; www.villabubion.com

GRANADA

HOTEL CARMEN (€€€)

Luxurious hotel in the centre of Granada, with all facilities. Special suites.

SAFETY AND SECURITY

Most types of accommodation in Andalucía have a watchful eye looking over them – if not the proprietor's, then a member of staff's. However, you should either take valuable items with you when going out, or make use of the establishment's safe, if it has one. If you have hired a car it is much more likely to be a target for theft. If you leave the car parked, ensure there is nothing visble on the back seat. Many *hostals* and hotels may have lifts without a closing cabin door, and the wall of the lift well is therefore unguarded as it travels up or down. Great care should be taken of young children in such lifts. If you have any legitimate complaint about your accommodation, ask for the *libro de reclamaciones* (official complaints book). This must be kept by law and should be inspected regularly by the police.

THE OLD, THE NEW AND THE LUXURIOUS

In cities there is a mix of old-fashioned and modern hotels. Hotels on the coast tend to be high-rise and modern. Top of the tree are *paradores*. These are state-run hotels, often located in magnificent buildings such as Moorish castles or palaces which have been luxuriously converted. Others are custom-built. All offer the highest standards and luxury, but have prices to match. If you want more remote accommodation with character, try the central booking service for cottages, farmhouses, refuges and other rural dwellings, the Red Andaluza de Alojamiento Rural ☎ 902 44 22 23; www.raar.es. As well as *paradores* there are state-run Villas Turistícas, complexes of luxury self-catering apartments or cottages that have all the central facilities of top hotels. For information contact Turismo Andaluz ☎ 952 12 93 00; www.andalucia.org

Pool terrace with great views. Jewellery and fashion shops for those with the money to spare.
✉ Acera del Darro 62 ☎ 958 25 83 00; www.hotelcarmen.com

HOTEL MACÍA PLAZA (€€)

Excellent location for visiting Granada's major attractions. Some rooms have a good view over this lively square.
✉ Plaza Nueva ☎ 958 22 75 36; www.maciahoteles.com

PARADOR DE GRANADA (€€€)

Top-of-the-range hotel – also top-of-the-hill – with its outstanding location at the heart of the Alhambra. Beautiful surroundings incorporate Moorish features. Reservations are strongly advised.
✉ Real de la Alhambra s/n ☎ 958 22 14 40; www.parador.es

GUADIX

HOTEL COMERCIO (€€)

Prize-winning hotel dating from 1901, beautifully refurbished. Comfortable rooms, lounges and restaurants serving top cuisine.
✉ Calle Mira de Amezcua, 3 ☎ 958 66 05 00; www.hotelcomercio.com

MOJÁCAR

PARADOR DE MOJÁCAR (€€€)

Luxurious hotel complex on Mojácar's seafront. The busy main road passes the gates and you have to cross this road to reach the far-from-

exclusive beach. However, the hotel has real exclusivity and luxurious facilities, including a swimming pool that you need never leave.
✉ Playa de Mojácar ☎ 950 47 82 50; www.parador.es

MONTEFRÍO

HOTEL LA ENREA (€€)

A very pleasant new hotel with modern facilities and excellent service.
✉ Paraje la Enrea s/n ☎ 958 33 66 62

SOLYNIEVE

MELÍA SIERRA NEVADA (€€€)

Most of Solynieve's hotels and *hostals* close during the summer and autumn, skiing being their main source of custom.
✉ Pradollano s/n ☎ 958 48 04 00; www.somelia.es

TREVÉLEZ

HOTEL LA FRAGUA (€€)

Well-placed hotel giving good views, with pleasant, well-appointed rooms. A bonus is the hotel's restaurant near by, the Méson la Fragua.
✉ Calle San Antoni 4 ☎ 958 85 86 26; www.hotellafragna.com

VÉLEZ BLANCO

HOSTAL LA SOCIEDAD (€)

Excellent value at this modern, well-appointed *hostal*. Enquire at the emphatically 'local' Bar Sociedad, in the main square, a few metres away.
✉ Calle Corredera 7 ☎ 950 41 50 27

Málaga & Cádiz

ANTEQUERA

PARADOR DE ANTEQUERA (€€)
Modern *parador* with all the luxury and good service associated with *paradors*. Surrounded by attractive gardens. Excellent restaurant and various activities, and excursions can be organised.
✉ Paseo García del Olmo s/n
☎ 952 84 02 61;
www.parador.es

ARCOS DE LA FRONTERA

HOTEL LA FONDA (€)
A delightful hotel in the busy lower town, but within easy reach of the old centre. La Fonda was originally a coaching inn, dating from the mid-19th century. Its restaurant is in the converted stables. High ceilings, wooden galleries and hand-made tiling all add to the atmosphere.
✉ Calle Corredera 83 ☎ 956 70 00 57; www.hotellafonda.com

LOS OLIVOS (€€)
Delightful, small hotel right in the heart of the old town. All modern facilities, yet with traditional style reflected in its beautiful patio. The hotel restaurant is recommended for excellent local cuisine.
✉ San Miguel 2, Boliches
☎ 956 70 08 11;
www.hotelolivosarcos.com

PARADOR DE ARCOS DE LA FRONTERA (€€€)
A prime location on the Plaza del Cabildo adds to the cachet of this luxury *parador*. Moorish and Mudéjar décor and furnishings throughout, and fine views from many of the balconied rooms. The restaurant serves traditional local cuisine.
✉ Plaza del Cabildo s/n
☎ 956 70 05 00;
www.parador.es

CADIZ

HOSTAL BAHIA (€)
Excellent-value small pension near the central Plaza de San Juan de Dios. Most rooms have balconies and all are attractively furnished with modern bathrooms. Recommended restaurant, Mesón La Nueva Marina, right next door.
✉ Calle Plocia 5 ☎ 956 25 90 61

HOSTAL FANTONI (€)
This delightful small *hostal* is tucked away in an otherwise dull side street off Plaza Juan de Dios. Marble staircases and *azulejos* tiles everywhere. Small but spotless rooms. Hugely popular, so reservations advised.
✉ Flamenco 5 ☎ 956 28 27 04

PARADOR HOTEL ATLÁNTICO (€€€)
Overlooking the sea and with direct access to the beach, this classic *parador* has all the luxurious facilities of its kind. Good restaurant offering traditional and international cuisine.
✉ Avenida Duque de Nájera 9
☎ 956 22 69 05;
www.parador.es

TRAVELLERS WITH DISABILITIES

There are few facilities for travellers with disabilities in Andalucía, but the situation may well improve as the authorities and the tourism business grow more aware of the need for them. It is already noticeable that more hotels are installing ramps, special lifts and other facilities for travellers with disabilities. For further information contact Las Gerencias Provinciales del Instituto Andaluz de Servicios Sociales (The Provincial Management of the Andalucían Institute of Social Services), Avenida Manuel Augustín 26, Málaga ☎ 952 12 96 00.

DRIVING MAZE

When looking for somewhere to stay in villages and small towns, resist the temptation to drive along ever-narrowing streets. If you are not sure where they are leading, you may end up like a cork in a bottle. If reversing round tight corners of narrow streets, check that the kerb is not as high as a small wall; otherwise the first you will know of it is a loud grinding noise. If you do get stuck across a narrow junction of village streets and no one is around, brace yourself. From all directions, a blaring cacophony of cars, vans, lorries, motorbikes, scooters, the occasional donkey plus amused pedestrians offering advice in quick-fire Spanish, is guaranteed to materialise within seconds.

GIBRALTAR

BRISTOL (€€)

A smart, mid-price hotel, but still near the top end for quality – like most things in Gibraltar. Near the cathedral, and with its own garden and pool.
✉ 10 Cathedral Square
☎ 350 76800

GRAZALEMA

VILLA TURÍSTICA DE GRAZALEMA (€€€)

Near the village of Grazalema, in fine surroundings, this luxury hotel is enhanced by its own gardens, pool and restaurant.
✉ Carretera. Comercal 344
☎ 956 13 21 36; www.tugasa.com

JEREZ DE LA FRONTERA

EL ANCLA HOTEL (€)

Delightful hotel in typical Andalucían building with wrought-iron balconies and yellow paint. Rooms are plain, but clean and comfortable.
✉ Plaza del Mamelón
☎ 956 32 12 97; www.hotel-ancia.com

MÁLAGA

LARIOS (€€€)

Smart hotel in the city centre's most fashionable shopping street. Black-and-white tiles, cool beige furnishings and pine make for a modern, upbeat look.
✉ Marqués de Larios 2
☎ 952 22 22 00; www.hotel-larios.com

MÁLAGA-GIBRALFARO (€€€)

Splendid *parador* high above the town on Gibralfaro hill, with glorious views over the bay.
✉ Castillo de Gibralfaro s/n
☎ 952 22 19 02; www.parador.es

NERJA

HOTEL BALCÓN DE EUROPA (€€)

At the heart of Nerja, adjoining the 'Balcón de Europa' and with access to Caletilla Beach.
✉ Paseo Balcón de Europa 1
☎ 952 52 08 00; www.hotelbalconeuropa.com

RONDA

HOTEL DON MIGUEL (€€)

A comfortable small hotel with pleasant rooms and some spectacular views of Ronda's famous gorge.
✉ Plaza España 4 ☎ 952 87 77 22; www.dmiguel.com

PARADOR DE RONDA (€€€€)

Ronda's 18th-century town hall now functions as a lavishly restored and delightful *parador*, with many of its rooms overlooking the Tajo, the deep gorge that has made Ronda famous.
✉ Plaza de España s/n ☎ 952 87 75 00; www.parador.es

ZAHARA DE LA SIERRA

ARCO DE LA VILLA (€€)

Small, modern hotel in an enviable position on Zahara's rocky outcrop. To reach it, go all the way through the village and then continue uphill towards the castle.
✉ Camino Nazari s/n ☎ 956 12 32 30

Seville & Huelva

ARACENA

FINCA VALBONO (€€)

In pleasant surroundings just outside Aracena, this old farmhouse has been tastefully converted into a small hotel with a pool, restaurant and riding stables.

✉ Carretera de Carboneras, Km 1 ☎ 959 12 77 11; www.fincavalbono.com

AROCHE

HOSTAL PICOS DE AROCHE (€)

It's worth the trip to Aroche for a stay in this friendly and immaculate establishment.

✉ Carretera Aracena 12 ☎ 959 14 04 75

CARMONA

PENSIÓN EL COMERCIO (€)

Attractive, small pension built into the walls of the Puerta de Sevilla, the magnificent western gateway to the town.

✉ Calle Torre del Oro 56 ☎ 954 14 00 18

HUELVA

LUZ HUELVA (€€€)

Top end of the price scale at this large, luxurious hotel near the museum and railway station.

✉ Alameda Sundheim 26 ☎ 959 25 00 11; www.nh-hoteles.com

MOGUER

HOSTAL PEDRO ALONSO NIÑO (€)

Outstanding value at this delightful little *hostal* with its immaculate tiled patio and comfortable en-suite rooms with TV.

✉ Calle Pedro Alonso Niño 13 ☎ 959 37 23 92

HOSTAL PLATERO (€)

Pleasant *hostal* named after the hero of Juan Ramón Jimenez's famous book and close to the centre of the town.

✉ Calle Aceña 4 ☎ 959 37 21 59

OSUNA

EL CABALLO BLANCO (€€)

This old coaching inn retains its arched entranceway and stable-yard, where guests park their cars. Pleasant rooms and good restaurant.

✉ Calle Granada 1 ☎ 954 81 01 84

SEVILLE

HOTEL ALFONSO XIII (€€€)

Expensive, luxurious hotel, custom-built in 1928 and still a focus of rich living. The stylised Moorish interiors are the last word in lavishness and there is an excellent restaurant.

✉ San Fernando 2 ☎ 954 91 70 00; www.alonsoxiii.com

HOTEL AMADEUS (€€)

Former 18th-century mansion, beautifully restored. With pianos in several soundproof rooms and concerts sometimes held in the foyer, this small hotel draws in musicians and music lovers. Terrace offers good views.

✉ Calle Farnesio ☎ 954 50 14 43; www.hotelamadeussevilla

PARKING

Many hotels and some *hostals* have their own parking, but finding a place to park in Andalucían towns and villages can sometimes be a nightmare. Car parks are either non-existent or obscure in most places, and central parking, especially in the mornings and late afternoons, is at a premium, amid quite hectic traffic. It is often best to find stress-free, street-side parking at the first convenient opportunity as you enter a town or village, depending on its size. This may entail a bit of a walk to the centre, but you can then assess more central parking and drive to it later.

Arts, Crafts, Gifts & Antiques

SOUVENIRS

Big cities and major attractions in Andalucía are well served by souvenir shops. Andalucía has a great tradition of craftwork, and in many quieter corners of cities, and certainly in provincial towns and villages, you will find shops, workshops and studios selling marvellous artefacts. For pottery and tiles, try Úbeda, Níjar and Sorbas. In Córdoba, look for Andalucían jewellery, the finest leather goods, guitars and embroidery. Jaén province is noted for wicker and woven crafts using esparto and other grasses; Úbeda also has several outlets, as does Guadix, in Granada province, and Almería city. Granada has numerous outlets for tapestry work and is also a noted centre of marquetry, a craft dating from Moorish times. Seville has many goldsmiths, silversmiths and potteries. You will find blankets and ponchos and other textile crafts at Grazalema and Níjar.

ART & CRAFTS

ALMERÍA

LA TIENDA DE LOS MILAGROS

This is one of the best places to go if you want to take home some of the distinctive local pottery produced by workshops in the Barrio Alfarero (Potter's Quarter).
✉ Calle Lavadero 2 (Níjar)
☎ 950 36 03 59

ARACENA

ARTESANÍA PASCUAL

A wonderful craft shop with a fascinating range of artefacts and potential gifts, and a friendly owner. You'll find it just behind the car park.
✉ Plaza de San Pedro 47
☎ 959 12 80 07

ARCOS DE LA FRONTERA

GALERÍA DE ARTE, ARX-ARCIS

Attractive gallery at the heart of the old town with a good selection of paintings, ceramics, esparto work, rugs and other traditional artefacts.
✉ Calle Marqués de Torresoto 11 ☎ 956 70 39 51

CARMONA

CERÁMICA SAN BLAS

Fine, working pottery tucked away down a quiet side street, complete with a modern pottery oven that radiates heat just inside the entrance door.
✉ Calle Domínguez de la Haza 18 ☎ 954 14 40 49

CÓRDOBA

BARAKA

The work of Córdoban artists is showcased at this arts and crafts shop in the Judería. Prices reflect the touristy location.
✉ Deanes, Manríquez s/n
☎ 957 48 83 27

EL ZOCO

A fascinating jewellery market in the heart of the Jewish quarter, with shops specialising in distinctive filigree silverware.
✉ Avenida de Gran Capitán
☎ No telephone

MERYAN

Córdoba was famed for its leatherwork. This shop is one of the few places where you can still buy traditional Córdoban leatherwork.
✉ Calleja de las Flores, 2
☎ 957 47 59 02;
www.meryancor.com

GRANADA

GONZÁLEZ RAMOS, TALLER DE TARACEA

One of the best workshop-galleries producing marquetry (taracea).
✉ Cuesta de Gomerez 12
☎ 958 22 20 70

LA TIENDA DE LOS MILAGROS

Ceramics with bright designs, skilfully blending traditional craft with modern ideas.
✉ Calle Lavadero 2 ☎ 950 36 03 59 (shop)

SEVILLE

MODAS MUÑOZ

The place for Sevillian

dress, if you fancy *mantoncillos*, flamenco veils, shawls and shoes to get your heels tapping.
✉ Cerrajería 5 ☎ 954 22 85 96

SARGADELOS

Spanish homewares, specifically beautiful Galician ceramics and other items, are sold in this gallery-outlet. The boldly patterned ceramics are made at Sargadelos's own factory in Spain. The shop also organises arts events and talks.
✉ Albareda 17 ☎ 954 21 67 08; www.sargadelos.com

SORBAS

ALFARERÍA JUAN SIMON

Family-run workshop and shop in the lower town, at the heart of the pottery-making district.
✉ Calle Alfarerías 25 ☎ 950 36 40 83

ÚBEDA

ALFARERÍA GONGORA

This well-known potter has his shop in the 'street of potters' in Úbeda – a town famous for its dark green pottery.
✉ Calle Cuesta de la Merced 32 ☎ 953 75 46 05

ALFARERÍA TITO

This shop in Úbeda's old town showcases the work of the Tito family, with Islamic-inspired vases and Andalucían glazes replicating the region's 16th-century pottery. Expect to pay for top quality.
✉ Plaza del Ayuntamiento 12 ☎ 953 75 13 02

GIFTS & ANTIQUES

GRANADA

CASA FERRER

Possibly the best-known music store in the province, dating from 1875; their stock includes an elegant assortment of hand-crafted guitars.
✉ Cuesta de Gomérez 26 ☎ 958 22 18 32

GONZÁLO REYES MUÑOZ

A fascinating antiques shop with a strong Spanish element. You'll find fine smaller pieces if you don't have room in your case for hefty furniture.
✉ Calle Mesones (Placeta de Cauchiles 1) ☎ 958 52 32 74

JUAN FAJARDO ANTIGUEDADES

An antiques shop in the Albaicín; if you're after a bronze of a bull or a kitsch crucifix, Juan will find something.
✉ Carrera del Darro 5 ☎ 696 510 940 (mobile)

RUIZ LINARES

A great mix of antiques and *objéts d'art* including paintings, sculptures, toys and jewellery.
✉ Calle Estribo 6–8 ☎ 958 22 23 47

SEVILLE

ARTESANÍA TEXTIL

Fascinating shop selling an intriguing selection of gift items, such as wall hangings and hand-embroidered tablecloths.
✉ Calle Sierpes 70 ☎ 954 56 28 40

BEGGING

You will need to get used to being approached in Andalucían cities by all types of people asking for money or cigarettes. Many beggars are businesslike, rattling through a crowded café terrace at a great pace, in order to avoid being seen off by quick-footed waiters, but also to cover as many people as possible. Outside major sights you may be approached by Gypsies offering sprigs of rosemary. If you do not wish to buy, do not engage in conversation or make eye contact; move on with purpose. As always, in crowded places, guard your pockets and bags.

Fashion & Books

LOCAL INFORMATION

Andalucía is becoming increasingly sophisticated in terms of tourism promotion, but there are sometimes huge variations in the kind of information available locally. Quite rightly, many areas of Andalucía cater for Spanish tourists first, and you may find that in some provincial towns and villages most, if not all, leaflets, brochures, local guidebooks and town and village maps are in Spanish, and that staff speak only Spanish. Many staff, however, do speak at least a little English.

FASHION

ALMERÍA

CARRUSEL
Shoes of all shades and styles for children are on offer in this bright and friendly little shop.
✉ Tenor Iribarne 11

CÓRDOBA

MODAS PILAR MORALES
A chic dress shop where assistants have just the right touch of Córdoban *hauteur*.
✉ Conde de Gondomar 2
☎ 957 47 12 54

GRANADA

ROBERTO VERINO
Very stylish, very cool fashion salon for both men's and women's wear.
✉ Alhóndiga 4
☎ 958 52 07 48

MÁLAGA

MANGO
Good-sized branch of this successful international chain. Well-made smart clothes, from snazzy suits to summer dresses
✉ Larios 1   ☎ 952 22 31 02

EL CORTE INGLÉS
Malaga's branch of Spain's venerable department store, good for almost anything.
✉ Avenida Andalucia 4–6
☎ 952 07 65 00

PUERTO BANÚS

DONNA PIU
Exciting fashions from Italian designer collections, to go with the general high fashion look in this trendy resort.
✉ Benabola   ☎ 952 81 49 90

SEVILLE

AGUA DE SEVILLA
Stylish perfumery and accessories shop tucked away in Santa Cruz.
✉ Rodrigo Caro 16
☎ 954 22 43 56

BOOKS

GRANADA

LIBRERÍA DAURO
A good little book shop with all types of books.
✉ Zacatin 3   ☎ 958 22 45 21

NERJA

NERJA BOOK AND VIDEO CENTRE
A big selection of second-hand books in various languages, as well as videos for rent.
✉ Calle Granada 32
☎ 952 52 09 08

SEVILLE

JUAN FORONDA
Delicate lace shawls, bright dresses and every imaginable flamenco accessory have been sold by Juan Foronda in this historic shop since 1926.
✉ Calle Tetuán 28 ☎ 954 22 60 60, www.juanforonda.com

VÉRTICE
International book shop in the university area of Seville. Maps, guides and general books in many languages.
✉ Calle San Fernando 33
☎ 954 21 16 54

Jewellery, Food & Drink

JEWELLERY

CÁDIZ

ARCO

This is one of those tucked-away shops with some appealing jewellery and accessories. It also does a charming line in mobile phones.

✉ Calle San José 23
☎ 956 22 30 71

FUENGIROLA

NICHOLSON

Fashionable jewellery products and accessories, including earrings and bracelets.

✉ Calle Marbella s/n
☎ 952 47 58 82

JEREZ

JOYERÍA MONACO

A wide selection of jewellery, gold and silver work, as well as porcelain and crystalware.

✉ Larga 17   ☎ 956 33 18 37

SEVILLE

CASA RUIZ

High-quality jewellery and silverware.

✉ O'Donnell 14   ☎ 954 22 21 37

FOOD & DRINK

ARACENA

JAMONES Y EMBEUTIDOS IBÉRICOS, LA TRASTIENDSA

The real *jamón negra* or *pata nergra* of the Sierra Morena is on sale here, as well as a range of other speciality Spanish meat products.

✉ Plaza San Pedro 2   ☎ 959 12 71 58

CÓRDOBA

MONSIEUR BOURGUIGON

A technicolour array of natural fruit sweets, handmade by Miriam García. Also fudge and nougat.

✉ Calle Jesús y Maria 11
☎ 656 33 02 80

GRANADA

LOPEZ-MEZQUITA

Mouth-watering and eye-catching displays in this *cafetería-pastelería* offering a huge array of sweet delicacies to tempt even the most jaded palate.

✉ Reyes Catolicos 39–41
☎ 958 22 12 05

GRAZALEMA

TODO SIERRA

This delicatessen is proudly stocked with products from the Sierra de Grazalema: preserves, oils, cheeses and hams.

✉ Plaza Andalucia 23
☎ 695 55 44 49

MÁLAGA

LA MALLORQUINA

One of the city's many wonderful delicatessens with a mouth-watering window display of great wheels of *Manchego* cheese, cold cuts, nuts, dried fruits and locally produced *turrón* (nougat) and marzipan. Also Málaga wine made from sweet muscatel grapes.

✉ Plaza de Félix Sáenz
☎ No phone

SPANISH FASHION

In the streets of Andalucía's main cities, and especially in stylish Seville, you will find fashion shops selling all the top brand names of Europe and America, as well as such increasingly known chains as Mango and Zara. For something essentially Andalucían, however, flamenco fashion is the ultimate. Though the flounced dresses in bright polka dot and floral patterns were once considered vulgar by Andalucían established society, today such costumes are proudly worn by countless Andalucíans during the great festivals and at numerous other events. The flamenco style is also replicated in contemporary fashion. You can buy items of flamenco costume in a number of shops, especially in Seville, Granada and Córdoba. But remember, it takes a certain panache to wear it well.

Nightlife & Flamenco

NIGHTLIFE

FLAMENCO

Flamenco is one of the enduring symbols of Andalucía. The frilly, brilliantly coloured dresses, the *batas de cola* worn by female dancers, the passionate intensity of singers, the rhythmic hand-clapping *jaleo*, the *staccato* footwork and sinuous movements of good dancers, all combine to produce one of the world's most exhilarating dance spectacles. It is hard to avoid this flamenco 'experience' in Andalucía, though it may not always be authentic. Experts will tell you, loftily, that the real thing erupts spontaneously, and only after midnight, in neighbourhood bars and in semiprivate *juergas* or all-night 'binges'. You may have to settle for a set piece 'flamenco evening' booked through hotels and tour operators. For details of performances of 'classical' flamenco by trained artistes, ask at Tourism Offices.

BENALMÁDENA COSTA

CASINO TORREQUEBRADA/ FORTUNA NIGHT CLUB
The place to come for Black Jack, roulette, poker, slot machines and a glitzy floor show. Passports must be shown at reception.
✉ Avenida del Sol ☎ 952 44 60 00 ⊙ Daily 9pm–4am

TIVOLI WORLD
There is a full range of musical entertainment here, including flamenco, country and western and popular musicals.
✉ Arroyo de la Miel ☎ 952 57 70 16

CADÍZ

EL MALECÓN
One of the most popular spots for Latin-style dancing.
✉ Paseo Pascual Pery ☎ 956 22 45 19

CÓRDOBA

LA ESTRELLA
Plaza de la Corredera is a large square enclosed by bars and clubs – La Estrella is just one of many venues, all of which stay open late. One of the most central destinations for nightlife in Córdoba.
✉ Plaza de la Corredera 14 ☎ 957 47 42 60 ⊙ Daily 11am–2am

GONGORA GRAN CAFÉ
This large multi-purpose venue, close to Plaza de las Tendillas, is open until the early hours and has a disco, bar and live music.
✉ Calle Gongora ☎ No phone ⊙ Mon–Sun 12pm–6/7am

FUENGIROLA

MOOCHERS JAZZ CAFÉ
Live music and giant pancakes are on offer in this popular jazz and Hollywood-themed bar-restaurant.
✉ Calle de la Cruz 17 ☎ 952 47 71 54

GRANADA

EL CAMBORIO
Swinging dance club with a young ambience. Very busy at weekends.
✉ Camino del Sacremonte ☎ No phone

MUSIC CLUB MILITANT POP
Modern pop club playing the latest indie bands and hip favourites – with a Britpop slant – in a small, dark room. Wednesday night is amateur DJ night.
✉ Rosario 10 ☎ No phone; www.fotolog.net/musikclub ⊙ Tue–Sat from 10.30pm

MARBELLA

CASINO MARBELLA
Blackjack, roulette, poker and slot machines. Passports must be shown at reception.
✉ Bajos del Hotel, Andalucia Plaza ☎ 952 81 40 00; www.casinomarbella.com ⊙ Slot machines 4pm–early hours. Casino 8pm–early hours. Restaurant 9pm–3am

OLIVIERE VALERES
Late-night venue decorated in mock Moorish style. Huge

dance floor and a variety of bars. Terrace for cooling off between sessions.

✉ Carretera Istan ☎ 952 82 88 61 ⏰ Daily 8pm–4am

SEVILLE

FUN CLUB

With all types of music, ranging from Latin American to jazz. Live bands at the weekend. A great place for dance enthusiasts.

✉ Alameda de Hércules 86 ☎ 650 48 98 58; www.salafunclub.com

FLAMENCO

BAEZA

PEÑA FLAMENCO

Occasional flamenco performances are staged here. Details from the tourist information office.

✉ Conde Romanones 6

CÓRDOBA

TABLAO CARDENAL

One of the best venues for 'classical' flamenco. Performances are staged in a delightful patio with an authentic ambience, opposite the Mezquita. Bar and restaurant service. Reservations advised.

✉ Calle Torrijos 10 ☎ 957 48 33 20; www.tablaocardenal.com

GRANADA

LOS TARANTOS

Touristy but fun flamenco show in the atmospheric setting of the caves of Sacramonte

✉ Camino del Sacramonte 9 ☎ 958 22 45 25 ⏰ Nightly from 9pm

JEREZ DE LA FRONTERA

FUNDACIÓN ANDALUZA DE FLAMENCO

Jerez is one of the great centres of flamenco and the Fundación performances are authentic 'classical' flamenco at its best.

✉ Plaza San Juan 1 ☎ 956 81 41 32

MÁLAGA

TEATRO MIGUEL DE CERVANTES

Regular flamenco shows are staged at this theatre and are of a good standard.

✉ Ramos Marín s/n ☎ 952 22 41 00

SEVILLE

EL ARENAL

A very lavish flamenco theatre and restaurant with stage shows, with or without meal. This is very much set-piece flamenco, but is well done and enjoyable. It caters mainly for coach parties, but individual reservations can be made, and you are advised to book if you want to go on your own.

✉ Calle Rodo 7 ☎ 954 21 64 92; www.tablaoelarenal.com ⏰ Daily 9pm, 11:30pm

LOS GALLOS

Although this is a smaller venue than El Arenal, it still has a good and lively atmosphere.

✉ Plaza de Santa Cruz ☎ 954 21 69 81; www.tablaolosgallos.com ⏰ Daily 9pm, 11.30pm

BULLFIGHTING

The *corrida de toros*, the bullfight, defines Spain as intensely as flamenco does. Both are viewed as art forms by the Spanish; both exhibit passion, pain and balletic elegance. Flamenco does not, however, involve the protracted torment and death of an animal, and it is this which defines bullfighting for most visitors as unequivocally cruel. The last thing you may want to see on holiday is a *corrida*, but it may be forced upon you on the television screens of countless bars, where it is watched by Andalucíans more intently at times than football. The bullfighting season runs from April to October and even some of the smallest villages stage *corridas* during their annual festivals. Larger towns and main cities have a programme of regular *corridas* that are usually prominently advertised.

Sports & Activities

HORSES

Horses and horseriding have a special appeal in Andalucía, the home of world-class horsemanship and open spaces. If you attend a big fiesta you will see horses and riders in all their finery. In remote villages, the ubiquitous presence of motorbike and scooter is often eclipsed, however momentarily, by the more melodious clatter of horses' hooves, as young riders from surrounding farms pass through, dusty from field and track. Throughout Andalucía, there are a number of riding schools that organise leisure rides and also give lessons in basic dressage and jumping skills. In the mountain areas, horse-trekking is a delightful way of seeing the Andalucían countryside.

BIRD WATCHING

PARQUE NACIONAL COTO DE DOÑANA

The Coto de Doñana National Park has a wealth of resident wildlife and migratory birds, the latter especially in spring and autumn. Four-wheel drive tours are available at the visitor centre.
✉ Doñana Visitor Centre
☎ 959 44 23 40; jeep tour reservations 959 43 04 32; www.discoveringdonana.com

EQUESTRIAN

DOÑANA ECUESTRE
Day-long rides through marshland.
✉ El Rocío, Parque Natural de Doñana ☎ 959 44 24 74; www.donanaecuestre.com

ESCUELA DE ARTE ECUESTRE 'COSTA DEL SOL'
Riding centre where you learn about the skills required to handle these famous Andalucían horses. Weekly dressage displays – Fridays in summer and Tuesdays in winter.
✉ Carretera 340, Km 159, Río Padrón Alto s/n, Estepona ☎ 959 44 24 66; www.escuela-ecuestre.com

HÍPICA INTERNATIONAL
Half-day rides available for experienced riders. Jumping and dressage lessons.
✉ Camino de la Sierra, Torremolinos ☎ 695 10 48 48

REAL ESCUELA ANDALUZA DEL ARTE ECUESTRE
The Royal Andalucían School of Equestrian Art is an unmissable experience. Even if horses are not your passion, they will become so during this superb display. Enjoy breathtaking equestrian movements in the Royal School's handsome arena.
✉ Avenida Duque de Abrantes, Jerez de la Frontera ☎ 956 31 96 35; www.realescuela.org
🕙 Mar –Oct Tue, Thu noon; Mar–Oct Mon, Wed, Fri 11, 1. Tours of stables and training sessions 💷 Expensive

GOLF

Visitors to Andalucía will find plenty of golfing opportunites.

ALHAURIN GOLF & COUNTRY CLUB
45 holes, par 72. Reasonable green fee.
✉ Mijas-Alhaurín el Grande, Málaga ☎ 952 59 59 70

ESTEPONA GOLF
18 holes, par 72. Reasonable fee.
✉ Apartado 532, Estepona ☎ 952 11 30 81

GOLF CLUB MARBELLA
18 holes, par 71. Expensive.
✉ Carretera de Cádiz, Marbella ☎ 952 83 05 00

GOLF TORREQUEBRADA
18 holes, par 72. Moderate fee.
✉ Carretera de Cádiz, N340, Banalmádena ☎ 952 44 27 42

LA QUINTA GOLF & COUNTRY CLUB
27 holes, par 72. Moderate fee.
✉ Carretera de Ronda, Km 3.5, Marbella ☎ 952 76 23 90

HANG-GLIDING/ PARAGLIDING

In the Valle de Abdalajís, near Málaga, thermal conditions are especially good for hang-gliding and paragliding.

CLUB VUELO LIBRE MÁLAGA

Week-long beginners courses available. Also two-seater flights with instructor.

✉ Valle de Abdalajis s/n
☎ 952 48 92 98

HOT-AIR BALLOOING

AVIACIÓN DE SOL

Organises hot-air balloon trips over land and sea.

✉ Apartado 344, Ronda
☎ 952 87 72 49

ADVENTURE SPORTS

EXTREME NATURE CAZORLA

Tour operator in Cazorla offering climbing, hiking, canoeing and other activities in the Sierra de Cazorla.

✉ Martinez Falero 52, Cazorla
☎ 649 39 38 31;
www.cazorlaextremenature.com

HORIZON

For the fit and the adventurous, Horizon offers a whole range of outdoor activities, including caving, rock-climbing, mountain-biking, paragliding and trekking, in the spectacular Sierra de Grazalema's Parque Natural.

✉ Calle Agua 5, Grazalema
☎ 956 13 23 63;
www.horizonventura.com

SKIING

SOLYNIEVE SKI RESORT

Europe's southernmost ski resort, with 86 runs in various levels of difficulty. Lively nightlife and many restaurants and bars.

✉ Southeast of Granada
☎ 902 70 80 90; www.cetursa.es

WATER SPORTS

BUCEO LA HERRADURA

Diving courses from 1- to 4-day programmes.

✉ Marine del Este, Almuñécar
☎ 958 82 70 83

CLUB NAUTICO DIVING CENTRE

Diving courses available all year at the Marina.

✉ Puerta Marina, Benalmádena s/n ☎ 952 56 07 69

PUERTO DEPORTIVO DE SAN JOSÉ

Diving in the protected Cabo de Gata Nature Park.

✉ San José, Cabo de Gata
☎ 950 38 00 41

TICKETS-TO-RIDE

Individual and group canoeing trips.

✉ Istán Lake, Istán (20 minutes from Marbella) ☎ 609 51 75 17

WINDSURFING

The Costa de la Luz has good windsurfing options.

CENTRO NAÚTICO ELCANO

✉ Prolongación de Ronda de Vigilancia s/n, Cádiz ☎ 956 29 00 12

CLUB MISTRAL

✉ Hurricane Hotel, Tarifa
☎ 956 68 90 98;
www.club-mistral.com

TOURIST INFORMATION

When looking for information on entertainment, events and other matters, you may find that the service at tourist information offices in main cities can be variable. At the big offices, staff who have to deal with a constant stream of enquiries sometimes seem to suffer from understandable 'enquiry fatigue'. In some rural towns and villages you may meet with apparent indifference. If you do not speak much Spanish, this, too, is understandable: many provincial tourism offices are used to dealing with mainly Spanish tourists. In other rural information offices you will be greeted by efficient and enthusiastic service. In very remote areas and isolated villages, the Ayuntamiento (Town Hall) is often the only source of information. At most town halls, you will be treated with kindness and, even in the absence of a shared language, people will do their best to help.

ANDALUCÍA
practical matters

WHAT YOU NEED

		UK	Germany	USA	Netherlands	Spain
● Required	Some countries require a passport to remain valid for a minimum					
○ Suggested	period (usually at least six months) beyond the date of entry –					
▲ Not required	contact their consulate or embassy or your travel agent for details.					
Passport/National Identity Card		●	●	●	●	●
Visa (regulations can change – check before you travel)		▲	▲	▲	▲	▲
Onward or Return Ticket		▲	▲	●	▲	▲
Health Inoculations		▲	▲	▲	▲	▲
Health Documentation (reciprocal agreement document: ➤ 90, Health)		●	●	▲	●	●
Travel Insurance		○	○	○	○	○
Driving Licence (national – EU format/national/Spanish trnsltn/international)		●	●	●	●	●
Car Insurance Certificate (if own car)		●	●	●	●	●
Car Registration Document (if own car)		●	●	●	●	●

WHEN TO GO

Average figures for Andalucía

■ High season
■ Low season

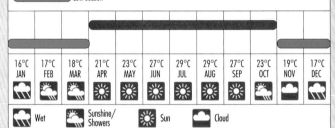

16°C JAN	17°C FEB	18°C MAR	21°C APR	23°C MAY	27°C JUN	29°C JUL	29°C AUG	27°C SEP	23°C OCT	19°C NOV	17°C DEC

☁ Wet ⛅ Sunshine/Showers ☀ Sun ☁ Cloud

TIME DIFFERENCES

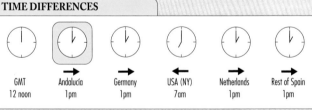

GMT 12 noon	Andalucía 1pm	Germany 1pm	USA (NY) 7am	Netherlands 1pm	Rest of Spain 1pm

TOURIST OFFICES

In the UK
Spanish Tourist Office,
22/23 Manchester Square,
London W1M 5AP
☎ 020 7486 8077
Fax: 020 7486 8034
www.spain.info
www.andalucia.org

In the USA
Tourist Office of Spain,
35th Floor, 666 Fifth Avenue
New York, NY 10103
☎ 212 265 8822
Fax: 212 265 8864
www.okspain.org

Tourist Office of Spain
8383 Wilshire Boulevard
Suite 960
Beverley Hills, CA 90211
☎ 323 658 7188
Fax: 3223 658 1061

ARRIVING

Almería Airport
Kilometres to city centre

8 kilometres

Journey times

 N/A

🚌 20 minutes

🚗 25 minutes

Málaga Airport
Kilometres to city centre

10 kilometres

Journey times

🚆 12 minutes

🚌 20 minutes

🚗 20 minutes

Seville Airport
Kilometres to city centre

8 kilometres

Journey times

🚆 N/A

🚌 20 minutes

🚗 20 minutes

TIME

 Spain is one hour ahead of Greenwich Mean Time (GMT+1), but from late March until the last Sunday in October, summer time (GMT+2) operates.

MONEY

Spain's currency is the euro (€) which is divided into 100 cents. Coins come in denominations of 1, 2, 5, 10, 20 and 50 cents, 1 and 2 euros, and notes come in 5, 10, 20, 50, 100, 200 and 500 euro denominations (the last two are rarely seen). The notes and one side of the coins are the same throughout the European single currency zone. Notes and coins from any EU countries can be used in Spain.

CUSTOMS

YES

From another EU country for personal use (guidelines)
800 cigarettes
200 cigars
1 kilogram of tobacco
10 litres of spirits (over 22%)
20 litres of aperitifs
90 litres of wine, of which 60 litres can be sparkling wine
110 litres of beer

From a non-EU country for your personal use, the allowances are:
200 cigarettes OR
50 cigars OR
250 grams of tobacco
1 litre of spirits (over 22 %)
2 litres of intermediary products (eg sherry) and sparkling wine
2 litres of still wine
50 grams of perfume
0.25 litres of eau de toilette

The value limit for goods is €240

Travellers under 17 years of age are not entitled to the tobacco and alcohol allowances.

NO

Drugs, firearms, ammunition, offensive weapons, obscene material, unlicensed animals.

CONSULATES

UK
☎ 952 35 23 00
(Málaga)

Germany
☎ 952 21 24 42
(Málaga)

USA
☎ 952 47 48 91
(Fuengirola)

Netherlands
☎ 952 27 99 54
(Málaga)

TOURIST OFFICES

Almería
Parque Nicolás Salmerón s/n
☎ 950 27 43 55

Baeza
Plaza del Pópulo s/n
☎ and fax 953 74 04 44

Cádiz
Avenida Ramón de Carranza s/n
☎ 956 25 86 46

Córdoba
Calle Torrijos 10
☎ 957 47 12 35

Granada
Corral del Carbón, Calle Libreras 2,
☎ 958 22 59 90
Municipal Tourist Office, Plaza Mariana
Pineda 10 ☎ 958 24 71 28

Huelva
Avenida de Alemania 12
☎ 959 25 74 03

Jaén
Maestra 13
☎ 953 24 26 24

Málaga
Pasaje de Chinitas 4
☎ 952 21 34 45

Ronda
Plaza de España 1
☎ and fax 952 87 12 72

Seville
Avenida de Kansas City s/n, Estación de
Santa Justa
☎ 954 53 76 26

Úbeda
Bajo de Marqués 4
☎ 954 75 08 97

NATIONAL HOLIDAYS

J	F	M	A	M	J	J	A	S	O	N	D
2	1	3	3	1	1	1	1		1	1	3

1 Jan	New Year's Day
6 Jan	Epiphany
28 Feb	Andalucían Day (regional)
Mar/Apr	Maundy Thursday, Good Friday, Easter Monday
1 May	Labour Day
24 Jun	San Juan (regional)
25 Jul	Santiago (regional)
15 Aug	Assumption of the Virgin
12 Oct	National Day
1 Nov	All Saints' Day
6 Dec	Constitution Day
8 Dec	Feast of the Immaculate Conception
25 Dec	Christmas Day

OPENING HOURS

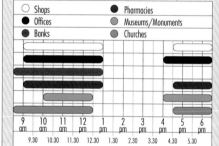

○ Shops	● Pharmacies
● Offices	● Museums/Monuments
● Banks	○ Churches

9 am	10 am	11 am	12 pm	1 pm	2 pm	3 pm	4 pm	5 pm	6 pm
9.30	10.30	11.30	12.30	1.30	2.30	3.30	4.30	5.30	

In addition to the times shown above, department stores, large super-markets and shops in tourist resorts open from 10am through to 8, 9 or even 10pm. The vast majority of shops close Sun and some close in Aug. Most banks open 9–2 Mon to Fri, some banks open 9–2 Sat. The times of museums is just a rough guide; some open longer in summer, while hours may be reduced in winter. Many museums close Sun afternoon, some also on Sat afternoon, as well as Mon or another day in the week. Some museums offer free entry to EU citizens (take your passport). Remember – all opening times are subject to change.

ELECTRICITY

The power supply is: 220/230 volts (in some bathrooms and older buildings:

110/120 volts). Type of socket: round two-hole sockets taking round plugs of two round pins. British visitors will need an adaptor and US visitors a voltage transformer.

TIPS/GRATUITIES

Yes ✓   No ✗

Restaurants (if service not included)	✓	5–10%
Cafés/bars (if service not included)	✓	change
Taxis	✓	2–3%
Tour guides	✓	change
Porters	✓	change
Chambermaids	✓	change
Hairdressers	✓	change
Restroom attendants	✓	change
Toilets	✓	change

PUBLIC TRANSPORT

Internal Flights The national airline, Iberia (www.iberia.com), plus the smaller Aviaco, operate an extensive network of internal flights. For reservations on domestic flights ☎ 902 40 05 00. Not cheap, but worth considering if in a hurry.

Trains Services are provided by the state-run company – RENFE (www.renfe.es). Fares are among the cheapest in Europe. For rail inquiries call Almería ☎ 950 23 18 22; Cádiz ☎ 902 24 02 02; Córdoba ☎ 902 24 02 02; Granada ☎ 902 24 02 02; Seville ☎ 902 24 02 02; Málaga ☎ 902 24 02 02; it is probably best to use only the central information line – ☎ 902 24 02 02 – because it has an English-language option.

Buses There is a comprehensive and reliable bus network operated by different companies along the coast and to inland towns and villages. Fares are very reasonable. Go to the local bus station for details of routes. Almería ☎ 950 26 20 98; Cádiz ☎ 950 21 00 29; Córdoba ☎ 957 40 40 40; Granada ☎ 958 18 54 80; Seville ☎ 954 41 71 11; Málaga ☎ 952 35 00 61.

Urban Transport Traffic in the cities of Andalucía generally and in the main towns and resorts of the Costa del Sol in particular, is normally heavy, especially in summer, but public transport in the form of buses is generally good.

CAR RENTAL

The leading international car rental companies operate in the main cities and on the Costa del Sol. You can hire a car in advance (essential at peak periods) either direct or through a travel agent. Hiring from a local firm can work out cheaper.

TAXIS

Only use taxis which display a licence issued by the local authority. Taxis show a green light when available for hire. They can be flagged down in the street. In cities and large towns taxis are metered; where they are not, determine the price of the journey in advance.

CONCESSIONS

Students/Youths Holders of an International Student Identity Card (ISIC) may be able to obtain some concessions on travel, entrance fees etc, but Andalucía is not really geared up for students (special facilities and programmes are limited). The main advantage for students and young people is that low-cost package deals are available.

Senior Citizens Andalucía is an excellent destination for older travellers – travel agents offer tailored package holidays. In winter there are special low-cost, long-stay holidays for senior citizens; the best deals are available through tour operators who specialise in holidays for senior citizens.

DRIVING

Speed limits on *autopistas* (toll motorways) and *autovías* (free motorways): **120kph**; dual carriageways and roads with overtaking lanes: **100kph**.

Speed limits on country roads: **90kph**

Speed limits on urban roads: **50kph**; in residential areas: **20kph**

Must be worn in front seats at all times and in the rear where fitted.

Random breath-testing. Never drive under the influence of alcohol.

Fuel (*gasolina*) is available in two grades; *Sin plomo* (unleaded, 95 and 98 octane); and gasoleo or *gasoil* (diesel). Petrol prices are fixed by the Government and are lower than those in the UK. Most garages take credit cards.

If you break down with your own car and are a member of an AIT-affiliated motoring club, call the Real Automóvil Club de España, or RACE (☎ 915 94 74 00; www.race.es) for assistance. If the car is hired you should follow the instructions in the documentation; most international rental firms provide a rescue service.

PHOTOGRAPHY

What to photograph: the rugged coast, unspoilt inland villages, examples of Moorish architecture, and panoramas of the Sierra Nevada.
Best times to photograph: the summer sun can be too bright at the height of the day, making photos taken at this time appear 'flat'. Take photographs in the early morning or late evening.
Where to buy consumables: film, camera batteries and digital cards are readily available from tourist shops, department stores and photo shops.

PERSONAL SAFETY

Snatching of handbags and cameras, pick-pocketing, theft of unattended baggage and car break-ins are the principal crimes against visitors. Any crime or loss should be reported to the national police force (Policía Nacional) who wear blue uniforms. Some precautions:
● Do not leave valuables on the beach or poolside
● Place valuables in a hotel safety-deposit box
● Wear handbags and cameras across your chest
● Avoid lonely, seedy and dark areas

Police assistance:
☎ **091**
from any call box

TELEPHONES

All telephone numbers throughout Spain now consist of nine digits and you must always dial all nine digits. Local calls are inexpensive. Although you can pay with coins, it is quicker and easier to buy a phonecard from any *estancos* (tobacconist). Many phones also take credit cards. Long-distance calls are cheaper from a booth than from your hotel. Directory information is 003.

International Dialling Codes

From Spain to:	
UK:	00 44
Germany:	00 49
USA:	00 1
Netherlands:	00 31

POST

Post Offices
Post offices (*correos*) are generally open as below; in main centres they may open extended hours. Málaga's main post office is at Avenida de Andalucía 1. Stamps (*sellos*) can also be bought at tobacconists (*estancos*). Open: 9–2 (1pm Sat); closed: Sun ☎ 902 19 71 97; www.correo.es (Málaga)

HEALTH

 Insurance
EU nationals can get some free medical treatment with the relevant documentation (EHIC card for Britons), although medical insurance is still advised and is essential for all other visitors. US visitors should check their insurance coverage.

 Dental Services
Dental treatment normally has to be paid for in full as dentists operate privately. A list of dentists can be found in the yellow pages of the telephone directory. Dental treatment should be covered by private medical insurance.

 Sun Advice
The sunniest (and hottest) months are July and August, when daytime temperatures are often into the 30°s C. Try to avoid the midday sun and use a high-factor sun cream to start with, and allow yourself to become used to the sun gradually.

 Drugs
Prescription and non-prescription drugs and medicines are available from pharmacies (*farmácias*), distinguished by a large green cross. They are able to dispense many drugs, which would be available only on prescription in other countries.

 Safe Water
Tap water is chlorinated and generally safe to drink; however, unfamiliar water may cause mild abdominal upsets. Mineral water (*agua mineral*) is cheap and widely available. It is sold *sin gas* (still) and *con gas* (carbonated).

LANGUAGE

Spanish is one of the easiest languages. All vowels are pure and short (as in English). Some useful tips on speaking: 'c' is lisped before 'e' and 'i', otherwise hard; 'h' is silent; 'J' is pronounced like a guttural 'J'; 'r' is rolled; 'v' sounds more like 'b'; and 'z' is the same as a soft 'c'. English is widely spoken in the principal resorts, but you will get a better reception if you at least try communicating with Spaniards in their own tongue.

hotel	*hotel*	breakfast	*desayuno*
room	*habitación*	toilet	*lavabo*
single/double	*individual/doble*	bath	*baño*
one/two nights	*una/dos noche(s)*	shower	*ducha*
per person/	*por persona/*	en suite	*en su habitación*
per room	*por habitación*	balcony	*balcón*
reservation	*reserva*	key	*llave*
rate	*precio*	chambermaid	*camarera*

bank	*banco*	foreign currency	*moneda extranjera*
exchange office	*oficina de cambio*	change money	*cambiar dinero*
post office	*correos*	pound sterling	*libra esterlina*
cashier	*cajero*	American dollar	*dólar estadounidense*
money	*dinero*	traveller's cheque	*cheque de viajero*
coin	*moneda*	giro cheque	*cheque postal*

restaurant	*restaurante*	snack	*merienda*
bar	*bar*	starter	*primer plato*
table	*mesa*	dish	*plato*
menu	*carta*	main course	*plato principal*
tourist menu	*menú turístico*	dessert	*postre*
wine list	*carta de vinos*	drink	*bebida*
lunch	*almuerzo*	waiter	*camarero*
dinner	*cena*	bill	*cuenta*

aeroplane	*avión*	ferry	*transbordador*
airport	*aeropuerto*	port	*puerto*
flight	*vuelo*	ticket	*billete*
train	*tren*	...single/return	*ida/ida y vuelta*
...station	*estación ferrocarril*	...first/second-class	*primera/segunda clase*
bus	*autobús*	timetable	*horario*
...station	*estación de autobuses*	seat	*asiento*
...stop	*parada de autobús*	non-smoking	*no fumadores*

yes	*sí*	help!	*ayuda!*
no	*no*	today	*hoy*
please	*por favór*	tomorrow	*mañana*
thank you	*gracias*	yesterday	*ayer*
hello	*hola*	how much?	*cuánto?*
goodbye	*adiós*	expensive	*caro*
good night	*buenas noches*	open	*abierto*
excuse me	*perdóneme*	closed	*cerrado*

REMEMBER

- Remember to contact the airport or airline on the day prior to leaving to ensure that the flight details are unchanged.
- There is no airport departure tax to pay, so you can happily spend your last remaining euros.
- Spanish customs are usually polite and normally easy to negotiate.

Index

TwinPack
Andalucía

Written by Des Hannigan
Updated by Robin Barton
Produced by AA Publishing
Editorial management Apostrophe S Limited
Designer Jacqueline Bailey
Series editor Cathy Hatley

A CIP catalogue record for this book is available from the British Library.

ISBN 978-0-7495-5539-9

Material in this book may have appeared in other AA publications.

Published by AA Publishing, a trading name of Automobile Association Developments Limited, whose registered office is Fanum House, Basing View, Basingstoke, Hampshire, RG21 4EA. Registered number 1878835.

© **AUTOMOBILE ASSOCIATION DEVELOPMENTS LIMITED 2008**
First published 2008

Colour separation by Keenes, Andover
Printed and bound by Everbest Printing Co. Limited, China

ACKNOWLEDGEMENTS
The Automobile Association would like to thank the following photographers, companies and picture libraries for their assistance in the preparation of this book. Abbreviations for the picture credits are as follows – (t) top; (b) bottom; (c) centre; (l) left; (r) right; (AA) AA World Travel Library.

1 AA/J Edmanson; 5t AA/J Tims; 5b AA/J Poulsen; 6 AA/M Chaplow; 7t AA/J Tims; 7b AA/ J Edmanson; 9 Jose Luis Gutierrez/Museo Picasso; 12 AA/J Tims; 13t AA/M Chaplow; 13b AA/J Tims; 14 AA/M Chaplow; 15 AA/P Wilson; 16 AA/ J Edmanson; 18 AA/M Chaplow; 19 AA/M Chaplow; 20l AA/D Robertson; 20r AA/M Chaplow; 21t AA/ J Edmanson; 21b AA/ J Edmanson; 23t AA/P Wilson; 23b AA/P Wilson; 24t AA/M Chaplow; 24b AA/M Chaplow; 25t AA/D Robertson; 25b AA/ J Edmanson; 26t AA/J Poulsen; 26b AA/P Wilson; 27 AA/ J Edmanson; 28t AA/D Robertson; 28b AA/D Robertson; 29t AA/D Robertson; 29b AA/D Robertson; 30t AA/A Molyneux; 30b AA/M Chaplow; 31t AA/M Chaplow; 31b AA/ J Edmanson; 32t AA/P Wilson; 32b AA/P Wilson; 33t AA/ J Edmanson; 33b AA/D Robertson; 34t AA/P Wilson; 34b AA/P Wilson; 35t Turespana; 35b Turespana; 36t AA/P Wilson; 36b AA/M Chaplow; 37t AA/ J Edmanson; 37b AA/M Chaplow; 38t AA/M Chaplow; 38b AA/ J Edmanson; 39 P Horree/Alamy; 40t travelstock44/Alamy; 40b P Titmuss/Alamy; 41t AA/D Robertson; 41b AA/M Chaplow; 42t AA/A Molyneux; 42b AA/A Molyneux; 43 AA/M Chaplow; 44t AA/ J Edmanson; 44b AA/A Molyneux; 45t AA/M Chaplow; 45b AA/P Wilson; 46t AA/M Chaplow; 46b AA/D Robertson; 47t AA/ J Edmanson; 47b AA/M Chaplow; 48t AA/M Chaplow; 48b AA/M Chaplow; 49t AA/ J Edmanson; 49b AA/W Voysey; 50 AA/M Chaplow; 51 AA/A Molyneux; 52 AA/ J Edmanson; 53 AA/P Wilson; 54 AA/J Poulsen; 55 AA/P Wilson; 56 AA/D Robertson; 58 AA/S Day; 59 AA/M Chaplow; 60 AA/A Molyneux; 61t AA/D Robertson; 61b AA/M Chaplow; 84 AA/A Molyneux; 85t AA/ J Edmanson; 85b AA/M Chaplow; 90bl AA/M Chaplow; 90tr AA/M Chaplow; 90br AA/M Chaplow. Front cover: Ape, Statue, AA/P Wilson; Boat, AA/J Tims; Woman, Plate, Casco Antiguo, Flower, AA/M Chaplow; Cuisine, AA/A Molyneux. Back cover, top to bottom: (a) AA/A Molyneux; (b) AA/M Chaplow; (c) AA/A Molyneux; (d) AA/D Robertson.

Every effort has been made to trace the copyright holders, and we apologise in advance for any accidental errors. We would be happy to apply the corrections in the following edition of this publication.

A03194
Cover maps produced from mapping © ISTITUTO GEOGRAFICO DE AGOSTINI S.p.A., NOVARA 2007, all rights reserved

TITLES IN THE TWINPACK SERIES
• Algarve • Andalucía • Corfu • Costa Blanca • Costa Brava • Costa del Sol • Crete •
• Croatia • Cyprus • Dubai • Gran Canaria • Lanzarote & Fuerteventura • Madeira •
• Mallorca • Malta & Gozo • Menorca • Provence & the Côte d'Azur • Tenerife •

Dear **TwinPack** Traveller

Your comments, opinions and recommendations are very important to us. So please help us to improve our travel guides by taking a few minutes to complete this simple questionnaire.

You do not need a stamp (unless posted outside the UK). If you do not want to cut this page from your guide, then photocopy it or write your answers on a plain sheet of paper.

Send to: **The Editor, AA TwinPack Travel Guides, FREEPOST SCE 4598, Basingstoke RG21 4GY.**

Your recommendations…

We always encourage readers' recommendations for restaurants, nightlife or shopping – if your recommendation is used in the next edition of the guide, we will send you a *FREE* **AA TwinPack Guide** of your choice. Please state below the establishment name, location and your reasons for recommending it.

_____

_____

_____

_____

Please send me **AA TwinPack**

Algarve ☐ Andalucía ☐ Corfu ☐ Costa Blanca ☐
Costa Brava ☐ Costa del Sol ☐ Crete ☐ Croatia ☐
Cyprus ☐ Dubai ☐ Gran Canaria ☐ Lanzarote & Fuerteventura ☐
Madeira ☐ Mallorca ☐ Malta & Gozo ☐ Menorca ☐
Provence & the Côte d'Azur ☐ Tenerife ☐
(please tick as appropriate)

About this guide…

Which title did you buy?

AA *TwinPack* _____

Where did you buy it? _____

When? m m / y y

Why did you choose an AA *TwinPack* Guide? _____

_____

_____

_____

Did this guide meet your expectations?

Exceeded ☐ Met all ☐ Met most ☐ Fell below ☐
Please give your reasons _____

_____

_____

continued on next page…

Were there any aspects of this guide that you particularly liked? _____

_____

_____

Is there anything we could have done better? _____

_____

_____

About you...

Name *(Mr/Mrs/Ms)* _____

Address _____

_____

_____ Postcode _____

Daytime tel no _____

Please only give us your mobile phone number if you wish to hear from us about other products and services from the AA and partners by text or mms.

Which age group are you in?

Under 25 ☐ 25–34 ☐ 35–44 ☐ 45–54 ☐ 55–64 ☐ 65+ ☐

How many trips do you make a year?

None ☐ One ☐ Two ☐ Three or more ☐

Are you an AA member? Yes ☐ No ☐

About your trip...

When did you book? m m / y y   When did you travel? m m / y y

How long did you stay? _____

Was it for business or leisure? _____

Did you buy any other travel guides for your trip?

If yes, which ones? _____

Thank you for taking the time to complete this questionnaire. Please send it to us as soon as possible, and remember, you do not need a stamp *(unless posted outside the UK)*.

Happy Holidays!